TIMOTHY P. SMITH

WITH BOB HOSTETLER

Foreword by Eugene Ulrich, PhD

THE
CHAMBERLAIN
KEY

**UNLOCKING THE GOD CODE TO REVEAL
DIVINE MESSAGES HIDDEN IN THE BIBLE**

WATERBROOK

This is a work of nonfiction. Nonetheless, the chronology of some events and conversations have been compressed. In addition, some of the names of the individuals involved have been changed. Any resulting resemblance to persons living or dead is entirely coincidental and unintentional.

Hardcover ISBN 978-1-60142-915-5
eBook ISBN 978-1-60142-916-2

Published in the United States by WaterBrook, an imprint of the Crown Publishing Group, a division of Penguin Random House LLC, New York.

WATERBROOK® and its deer colophon are registered trademarks of Penguin Random House LLC.

Library of Congress Cataloging-in-Publication Data
Names: Smith, Timothy P., 1955– author.
Title: The chamberlain key : unlocking the biblical code that proves the existence of God / Timothy P. Smith, with Bob Hostetler.
Description: First Edition. | Colorado Springs, Colorado : WaterBrook, 2017. | Includes bibliographical references and index.
Identifiers: LCCN 2016051192 (print) | LCCN 2017006796 (ebook) | ISBN 9781601429155 (hardcover) | ISBN 9781601429162 (electronic)
Subjects: LCSH: Bible—Criticism, interpretation, etc. | Bible—Prophecies. | Symbolism in the Bible.
Classification: LCC BS511.3 .S625 2017 (print) | LCC BS511.3 (ebook) | DDC 220.6/8—dc23
LC record available at https://lccn.loc.gov/2016051192

Printed in the United States of America
2017—First Edition

10 9 8 7 6 5 4 3 2 1

SPECIAL SALES

Most WaterBrook books are available at special quantity discounts when purchased in bulk by corporations, organizations, and special-interest groups. Custom imprinting or excerpting can also be done to fit special needs. For information, please e-mail specialmarketscms@penguinrandomhouse.com or call 1-800-603-7051.

This book is dedicated to all the parents in the world—past, present, and future—whether by blood, adoption, or unofficial arrangement. There is something about parenthood that seems to both challenge and reward every facet of our humanity and allow all those who take this responsibility upon themselves to discover the full dimensions of their own nature. It is also dedicated especially to my own parents, who have lived to see the love they have shared with each other blossom like "a fruitful bough, even a fruitful bough by a well; whose branches run over the wall" (Genesis 49:22, KJV).

CONTENTS

CONTENTS

PART IV: SIGNS AND WARNINGS

FOREWORD

As chief editor of the biblical Dead Sea Scrolls, I have spent my entire career teaching and writing in the areas of the Hebrew Scriptures, the scrolls, and the Septuagint. With regard to the reliability of the Masoretic Hebrew text that is used in the observations made in this book, it is based on the Saint Petersburg Codex (*Codex Leningradensis; Firkovich B 19 A*), which is the oldest complete manuscript of the Hebrew Bible in the Hebrew language, whose colophon dates it to AD 1008 or 1009. This is the text, in modern printed form (*Biblia Hebraica Stuttgartensia*), used by most scholars today.

The Aleppo Codex is almost a century older, but most of the Pentateuch is missing from it. The Dead Sea Scrolls are older by a millennium, but, though fragments from almost thirty manuscripts containing parts of Genesis are preserved, none contains text from Genesis 30.

The antiquity of that Hebrew tradition is safely assured, however, by three different sources. First, the Dead Sea Scrolls in the Genesis fragments that did survive exhibit a text that is virtually identical with the Saint Petersburg Codex. Second, the (pre-Christian) Samaritan Pentateuch is identical with it in its consonantal text. Third, the ancient Greek translation (the Septuagint) of Genesis, most scholars would agree, was translated around 280 BC from a Hebrew source text that was virtually identical with the Hebrew consonantal text of the Leningrad Codex.

However one wishes to interpret the meaning and significance of this book, the reader may rest assured that the text on which Timothy Smith bases his interpretation has almost certainly been there for a very long time, since before the birth of Christ.

—Eugene Ulrich, PhD
Chief Editor, Biblical Dead Sea Scrolls
Department of Theology, University of Notre Dame

Out of the Shadows

F or more than fifteen years I managed to keep the lid on a discovery that will dramatically redirect biblical scholarship, Christian theology, and perhaps even the trajectory of history itself.

What began as a mystery concerning my own family and ancestry has unfolded into perhaps the most astounding revelation of the modern age, as you will see in the pages that follow. It is based on an unexplained phenomenon, an anomaly in four verses of text in the oldest complete manuscript of the Hebrew book of Genesis. I have found messages embedded in those few verses that simply could not be there— but nevertheless they were.

I have pursued every possible explanation in an effort to account for this bizarre finding. One discovery has led to another and then another. I've consulted some of the world's most respected scholars and scientists until only one plausible explanation remains: the original ancient text of the Hebrew Scriptures (parts of which date back to 800 BC, perhaps earlier) is more than a text in the traditional sense—more than a manuscript containing wisdom and prophecy and transcendent truth. It is also a complex communication device with the ability to breach the very boundaries of time itself. By using this tool, a supernatural power has reached across millenniums to make contact with you and me, right here and now.

The text of the Hebrew Bible presents us with a familiar literary structure.

Words form sentences and concepts that we recognize. We use accepted rules of translation and interpretation to extract what we believe is the meaning of the narrative. However, the smallest discrete units of the biblical text are Hebrew letters, the quanta of this textual universe, which are capable of organizing themselves into a less obvious form of intelligent communication, one that transcends the ordinary parameters of time and space. This hidden substructure is what holds the ancient Hebrew text together.

The key that I've found to this hidden language is not some rigid, mechanical cipher code but a means of gaining access to the beautifully unpredictable nature of the universe and life itself, which turns out to possess a level of order that is both intentional and intelligent. A manifestation of divine intelligence—or God, if you will—is functioning in visible ways right alongside us.

And now we have a new way to access it.

It is no easy task to explain how I made this discovery, let alone to help you understand and believe it. After all, I am neither a scholar nor a theologian. Neither am I an expert in ancient languages. In some ways I am a most unlikely candidate to have uncovered signs of a divine hand at work, which sometimes has left me wondering, *Why me?* and *Why now?*

I hope the account you are about to read will answer those questions while also serving to strengthen your faith, as it has mine.

PART I

THE UNFOLDING

Finder of Lost and Hidden Things

Virginia, 2016

The chamberlain key was not my first discovery in a life marked by curiosity and exploration. But it is by far the most important and consequential.

For more than thirty years I have engaged in the work of evaluating and preserving valuable physical objects from every part of the world and every period in history. I have spent most of my life answering questions and unraveling mysteries, many of which began with something I could touch: a chest, a painting, a tapestry, a scepter, a banner, a coin, a cloak, a sword, or a scroll. As an appraiser, restorer, and conservator of fine art and antiquities, I have discovered priceless items stashed in attic eaves, sealed in long-forgotten vaults, or gone missing from the White House. Many such treasures have impressed me with their astronomical value, dazzled me with their breathtaking beauty, or haunted me with their gruesome history. But like many explorers, historians, and investigators, I have passed much of my time in the unglamorous drudgery of countless details, the disconnected bits of things that must be carefully considered, culled, and reassembled before the destination is reached or the truth uncovered.

My paternal grandfather, Clarence R. Smith, arrived in Washington, DC, in 1938 to begin the construction of the Jefferson Memorial. He also worked on a number of other important building and renovation projects: the National Gallery of Art, the US

Capitol, the Carderock Division of the Naval Sea Systems Command, and many others. His youngest son—my father, E. Jay Smith—continued in this tradition, beginning with the construction of the official residence of the vice president on the grounds of the US Naval Observatory. When my father retired in the 1990s, his building and architectural firm was credited with designing, building, and renovating many of the Washington area's most venerated public buildings and private residences.

I was born in 1960 in Langley, Virginia, a tiny community just inside the Washington, DC, Beltway. In 1966 my parents purchased a small horse farm in Great Falls, Virginia, a mere seven miles up the Potomac from Langley. The place was called Windswept, and all the horses had been named accordingly: Gusty, Breezy, Sea Breeze, and so on. The brick ranch house rambled along the side of a steep hill overlooking rolling pastures and a lake fed by a stream known as Colvin Run. The property was adjoined on all sides by other horse farms and small Virginia estates.

Among my favorite activities on a cold, rainy day was to sneak into our home's spacious attic and pull up the ladder behind me so no one would know I was there. I listened to the muffled sound of voices and footsteps below, delighted by the musty secrecy of the place, as I rummaged through boxes of old photographs, sports equipment, toys, tools, and Christmas decorations. I set up the family nativity scene, placing a small candle in the stable, positioning and repositioning animals and people until I was satisfied that all were in their correct spots.

One stormy day in late winter I could no longer resist the sturdy pine boxes stacked against the eaves in the far corner of the attic. I knew perfectly well they were forbidden, but their lure was overpowering. By the light of a red Christmas candle I carefully slid the top crates onto the attic floor, opened them one by one, and inspected their contents. There were folders full of old handwritten documents, their pages creased and oxidized to a light tobacco brown. One box contained nothing but ornate knobs, handles, and latches—some of rich patinated brass and others of skillfully handwrought iron, pitted and rusted but still intact. Another was crammed with metal tubes containing rolled-up architectural drawings and wonderful hand-colored maps that I turned in every direction, attempting to decipher their locations in the larger world.

Most curious of all was a large iron star, cast in round relief, its dry soldier-blue paint flaking off onto my hands as I dragged it into the candlelight for a better look. I hefted it above my head and figured it weighed more than half a sack of sweet feed, about thirty-five pounds. I had no idea at the time where it had come from and what its purpose might have been. Only later would I learn that it was originally part of a set of thirteen, one star for each of the original American colonies.

I would also discover that twenty years before, at the end of World War II, my grandfather had begun one of many renovation projects on the US Capitol building, this time to replace the ceilings and roofs of both the House and Senate chambers. The star I'd found in the attic once hung in the Capitol but had since become part of a forgotten treasure trove of historic documents and artifacts in that structure's attics and catacombs. As the only star among its companions that was ever salvaged and retrieved, in some ways it illuminated the course of my professional life and personal passion. Years later, when I became a professional hunter and finder and restorer of lost and forgotten things, I arranged for the star to be returned to the architect of the Capitol.

A TREASURE HUNTER'S TRAINING

On the first day of my summer vacation from school in 1972, my dad came into my bedroom at 5:30 a.m. and placed a leather tool belt, fully equipped, at the foot of my bed and told me it was time to get up and get going. This was not a total surprise, since all three of my older brothers had their summer vacations commandeered in the same way. I spent my first day "on the job" at the equipment and material yard, where I worked in the blazing sun, prying nails out of old lumber so it could be reclaimed for concrete forms, scaffold boards, and gangways. My supervisor, Lonnie, was a tough, weathered African American man who had worked for my father since my father first went into business and with my grandfather before that. Under his watchful eye I hauled bricks, mortar, lumber, and shingles from one spot to another and occasionally swung my hammer at wide-headed roofing nails that Lonnie must have figured were hard to miss.

Toward the end of that summer, a plan began to shape itself in me. I recognized that it wasn't the buildings themselves that interested me, despite their magnificence;

it was the things we often found in them. Some of the workmen, including my older family members, spoke of finding old and curious items in strange places, and I began to wonder if a job existed where a person could be paid to locate lost or hidden objects, a sort of professional finder of things.

By the time I was twenty years old, I owned and operated a thriving antique-restoration operation out of the family-business headquarters in McLean, Virginia. Capitalizing on the reputations of my father and grandfather, I was invited into homes and institutions that were pretty heady for someone my age. I hired the most talented and dependable subcontractors in the area: oil-painting conservationists trained at the Royal Academy of Arts in London, porcelain specialists from China, cabinet and furniture makers moonlighting from their jobs with my father, and a furniture upholsterer who had worked for every First Lady since Bess Truman. I ferried the more common items to a workshop I maintained in the Shenandoah Valley. I plied everyone I encountered for information, techniques, and trade secrets, learning how to handle many projects myself. I trained others from scratch to handle the nuts-and-bolts repair jobs, and I developed protocols and habits that serve me well to this day.

Not long after setting up my own shop, I was invited to perhaps the most historic estate home in the McLean area. Known as Salona, it had been the home of Henry "Light Horse Harry" Lee, the Revolutionary War hero and father of Gen. Robert E. Lee. The current owner was a distinguished elderly woman, matriarch of a prominent Mid-Atlantic political family. We had never met, but she contacted me because she knew my parents socially and because my father's company had been involved in the architectural renovation of Salona House.

When she greeted me at the door, I got the impression that she mistook me for my oldest brother (I sported a closely trimmed beard at the time and looked older than my twenty years). As she led me on a grand tour of the historic home, it was obvious she had played the docent many times before.

My hostess began by describing a pre-Columbian settlement on the site and showed me a small collection of Native American artifacts that had been unearthed on the property over the years. She led me from room to room, recounting well-rehearsed facts and anecdotes about the furnishings and architectural details of the estate home. Nearly every piece of English and Early American furniture had a story that was interwoven with important events in Virginia history and the many prominent figures in her family. She identified the subject of every portrait on the walls and drew my attention to antique Persian carpets, rare Chinese Imperial and imported porcelains, delicate English Staffordshire pieces, and sturdy mocha-ware pottery. She concluded her private seminar with a romantic (and historically accurate) account of how Dolley Madison fled to the refuge of Salona in 1814 when British troops were burning the White House in order to reunite with her husband, President James Madison, who had arrived the previous day.

Having completed the tour, we reversed our course back through the house as my hostess pointed out various furnishings, artwork, and other items I would be asked to clean, repair, and restore. She never requested a cost estimate, only a timeline for completing the work. Though at the time I was in over my head, I took great pains with those valuable articles and learned all I could about them while they were in my care: the precise materials used in their composition, the methods applied to their construction, individual variations and subtleties of style and proportion, as well as the identity and background of their makers. I consulted with seasoned experts to be sure I didn't embark on any process that might depreciate the pieces in any way. I was especially keen to note signs of previous restoration and repair, to avoid the less-than-perfect work of my predecessors in the trade, and to emulate their most artful successes.

That was a seminal experience for me. The care and effort I invested in Salona House soon brought more opportunities, and I gave every new assignment as much attention as I had the first, along with the benefit of my growing expertise. I made it my goal to turn up some new tidbit of information that I could offer every client when the job was finished and their precious objects returned. My patrons appreciated my interest and enthusiasm, and they rewarded me with referrals that led to a constant stream of fascinating employment.

By the time I was twenty-six years old, I was operating one of the largest antique and fine-art restoration businesses in North America, with one division devoted to private clients and another to contracts with the federal government.

But the clues to the greatest treasure I would ever discover were still hidden in my dreams.

STORMS AND SYMBOLS

My life on the surface no doubt looked great to outsiders, but my inside life was a different story. I was experiencing a crisis of faith. Although my family, church, and business responsibilities were expanding and thriving, my spiritual strength seemed to be draining away. Was I buckling under my new responsibilities? Was I burning out? Cracking up?

My dreams were contributing to my stress. On the exact same date for three years in a row—beginning on the night of January 12, 1986—I'd had the same powerful dream. I know because I started keeping a journal the morning after the first one, a practice I have continued ever since.

Each dream began the same way, with a massive dark storm rising ominously on the horizon, but the dream each year extended the story and contributed new details. These dramatic scenes employed distinct symbols, some of which were familiar to me and some of which were entirely new. After each dream I dug into Scripture and history to try to decipher its meaning.

Then one night in April 1989 I had another dream, this one out of sequence and very different from the rest, a dream in which I was looking at a map of North America. I saw a tiny cartoon version of our Ford van driving from east to west across the continent, much like a 1940s newsreel showing a plane flying across a spinning globe. In the dream our van stopped deep in the Canadian Rockies of British Columbia. The location imprinted itself so vividly in my brain that when I awoke I was able to pull out an atlas and mark the spot. I noted the longitude and latitude, wrote them down on a scrap of paper, and put it in my wallet.

I believed, because of the repetitive nature of the dreams and some of the symbolic nature of the content, that I was being guided—and prompted to act—though for what purpose I didn't have a clue. Thanks to the dream, however, I did have one strikingly specific detail: a place I could locate.

Plunging ahead with the reckless confidence—and often the foolishness—of youth, I decided to go there.

An Overwhelming Encounter

Western Canada, 1989

In the summer I drove my family to British Columbia and the location indicated in my dream, four hundred miles north of Fort Saint James, high in Canada's Rocky Mountains. My wife was just a few months from delivering our third son. Our two other sons, ages four and six, sported coonskin caps, assuming we were on a marvelous wilderness adventure. A friend of mine and his wife were also traveling with us.

Strange things started happening from the moment we arrived in mid-July. Maps showed nothing at the longitude and latitude I'd so carefully recorded. No towns, no roads, no camps—nothing at all. I had never been high in the Rockies before, especially this far from civilization. It was breathtakingly beautiful but also more than a little frightening. We were able to access the location only via an old logging road often blocked by fallen limbs or bisected by tumbling streams that required us to carefully negotiate the best way to get our Ford van across. We had brought along sufficient supplies to get through the winter, and both women were slowly coming to the realization that I was crazy enough to proceed with my plan to winter there (winter temperatures in that part of the Canadian Rockies can plummet to fifty degrees below zero).

When we reached the precise spot I was looking for, a spectacular panorama opened before us. Two aquamarine lakes, one feeding into the other, reflected the surrounding wilderness in every direction, looking as pristine as the day it was created. To the northwest one majestic peak towered above the rest, and no sooner had we stepped from the van to take in the scene than a vivid rainbow appeared over it. The sight was stunning, a sign perhaps, but what it might mean other than "Welcome, traveler," I had no idea.

We set up a camp of two dome tents protected by large tarpaulin canopies, under which we arranged folding chairs, clothes-drying racks, and other simple necessities. The boys gathered several dozen large, smooth stones from a nearby stream, and we fashioned a deep circular fire pit. Once we started a blazing fire, we dove into the lake for a frigid but long-overdue bath.

The next day I climbed as high into this mountain as daylight in those northern latitudes would permit. The responsibility for my family and companions weighed heavily on my mind and soul as I built a small fire with the limited forage available this high above the tree line. I intended to stay on Rainbow Mountain (as I now called it) as long as it took to receive some kind of divine guidance. Having come this far, I needed to understand why I had been summoned to this spot and how my wife could safely give birth in such a place. Within a few months there would be no getting out, and I worried that our camping supplies would be no match for winter in the wilderness.

I stayed that night on Rainbow Mountain huddled close to a small fire, pouring out my heart and soul to God. At daybreak I returned to camp with hardly a whispered promise or intimation of peace. In truth I was confused and disillusioned as well as exhausted from the arduous hike and the cold, sleepless night. I promptly fell asleep in our tent only to experience a vivid dream. My family, friends, and I were welcomed by a large group of people (who were somehow related to one another) to a lovely cabin on a farm near the banks of a crystal river. The hand-hewn logs of the cabin and its surroundings were clear in every detail, including the cabin's furnishings.

When I awoke I carefully recorded the dream in my journal and described it to my wife and friends. I told them that if such a place actually existed, I would recognize it instantly.

Shelter from the Storm

Our campsite in Rainbow Valley marked the end of a trail; there was no going forward in a vehicle, so in order to search for the cabin I had seen in my dream, we had to work our way back the way we came. In ten miles or so we reached a logging road that roughly followed the course of the Omineca River. Having already traversed the side heading toward Germansen Landing, we turned upriver. This road, in better shape than our Rainbow Valley trail, twisted and turned as it followed the river's meanderings. We saw two other cabins as we drove upriver, and the rest of the party insisted we stop and investigate them. But neither looked anything like the site in my dream, so we kept going. The rough road wound down a long grade and then rose as it hugged the Omineca, when suddenly the cabin I had seen in my dream just twenty-four hours earlier appeared on our left.

We piled out of the van to inspect the sprawling homestead that obviously belonged to someone who had not been there in some time. The five-acre clearing that revealed a bend in the swiftly flowing Omineca River was nestled in an alpine landscape of massive fir trees interspersed with alders whose trunks looked like bleached bones. In the mountains that surrounded us, flora eventually gave way to barren rock slides and snow-tipped peaks. As my two small sons dashed about the compound calling out one exciting discovery after another, the grown-ups poked around the main cabin.

It was a simple log structure consisting of a kitchen, a great room, and two small bedrooms off to one side. Above these was an additional low-pitched loft that I knew immediately would be perfect for the boys, accessible by a crude ladder. A wood-fired cookstove in the kitchen and a potbellied stove in the center of the structure promised ample heat. A lean-to pantry off the back of the kitchen was equipped with a primitive indoor privy that was a warmer prospect for the upcoming winter than midnight walks in the snow to an outhouse. Two other one-room cabins dotted the clearing as well as a large woodshed, a dilapidated barn and chicken coop, and a workshop close to the old logging road that continued into the wilderness of the Northwest Territories.

It was everything I had seen in my dream, except no one was here to welcome us. And although we had explored freely so far, we couldn't just move in without permission from the cabin's owners. So we piled back into our van and drove several miles back down the rugged logging road to Germansen Landing, just beyond the bridge that spanned the Omineca River. It was the closest thing to civilization in the area, a trading post for miners, loggers, trappers, and the few homesteading families that we learned were spread over hundreds of square miles in the surrounding wilderness. We asked the family that tended the little store about the vacant property and learned that it belonged to a family from Alberta that was due to arrive soon on their annual family getaway. We returned to the homestead, set up camp near the river, and awaited the family's arrival.

In less than a week they showed up, and all eleven of them — children included — were die-hard wilderness survivalists. Informed about our presence by the proprietors of the trading post, they acted as if it were the most natural thing in the world for us to be waiting for them on their property. The encounter was surreal yet comforting. They invited us to move into one of the smaller cabins and make ourselves comfortable. No one among them was much of a talker, but for the next three weeks our new friends made it their mission to pass on their catalog of knowledge and skills: hunting, fishing, trapping, gathering, and foraging, as well as an awareness of the area's many dangers. I was content to enjoy their company and learn all I could while planning to ask a favor that seemed too much to ask. It turned out I never had to make my request.

A few days before their sojourn's end, Frank, patriarch of the clan, asked me to walk with him down by the river where he had first taught us to hunt grouse. This time, however, he left his bird gun behind. The extended August sun warmed the afternoon and sparkled off the river. I followed him without conversation or question, waiting for him to speak his mind.

"I understand you folks intend to stay out here. You're looking for something, and you think you might find it here."

I knew he wasn't asking a question. "That's true, although what I'm looking for isn't something you can lay your hands on."

"That's a good sort of thing to be seeking." He sounded satisfied with my answer.

I was tempted to tell him what had led me out here in the first place, including my dreams, but the situation was complicated, and I didn't want to speak for anyone else. My friends had their own ideas, which seemed to change regularly, and my wife had tentatively agreed to the trip, but naturally her first concern was the safety and welfare of our children—including the baby who was due in the middle of winter. *I should never have encouraged anyone to come with me,* I thought. "This was all my idea."

"I figured as much." He nodded and looked across the river at a swarm of black flies on the opposite shore. "The breeze is holding them over there for now, but if it shifts, they'll be all over us." This was no casual warning—the mosquitoes and black flies in that part of the Rockies were vicious at this time of the year—but I sensed something deeper in his observation.

"Things would be simpler if I had come alone. This place is beautiful, but I know it can get harsh." I was trying to sound sensible.

"Yep. I've been bringing my family out here at all times of year. They like it for the most part, especially the boys. Never had anything really bad happen. A few close calls. You all can stay right here for as long as you like." With one last wary glance at the flies, Frank turned and headed up the trail back toward the cabins.

I said nothing but stayed right on his heels.

"You've got most of what you need to get through the winter. I know you got a ton of that freeze-dried food, but I'd get a pile of onions and potatoes from the trading post if I were you. You can trap hares and ice-fish too. Don't imagine you're going to bring down a moose with the peashooter I'm going to leave you, but it's good for grouse. There's a few folks around here you can count on in a pinch. You'll meet 'em, and they'll drop by.

"Here's the most important thing: when the first big snow hits, which will be sooner than you think, you and that friend of yours get the two big square-point shovels in the tool shed and bank up snow against the side of the cabin, all the way up to the top of the walls. Bank it and pack it. Don't worry about the roof; it'll take care of itself. You're going to turn that cabin into an igloo. If you do like I say, that old wood stove will keep that place so warm it'll near chase you out no matter how cold it gets." He glanced back at me. "You got all that?"

"Yes, sir. I understand. And I really appreciate it. That's a load off my mind."

"Good. And one more thing." Without breaking stride he said, "You'll find what you're looking for sooner or later. In the meantime, you keep your family warm and fed."

Though we had become friends over the previous three weeks, Frank's generosity astounded me. And thanks to his advice we did stay warm and well fed. That remote cabin on the banks of the Omineca River became a sacred place for me, the site of miracles and wonder. I experienced for the first time in my life what it was like to survive on one of our planet's outer edges, where so much of God's creation still supplies both sanctuary and danger, often in dizzying succession.

My third son would be born there that December, delivered right into my own hands, after my wife endured an extended and exhausting labor. I would learn how to pray with desperate humility and would experience the swiftness of God's provision when we turned to Him in dire circumstances. I would discard many cherished misconceptions, toted into the mountains with the rest of my gear. I would experience many powerful dreams and visions, but none compared to what occurred one September night when the northern lights were crackling and blazing in a flawless starlit sky.

A Night to Remember

The wee hours of September 8, 1989, changed my life forever in ways I could not yet begin to imagine. God heard my prayers and answered my yearning in such a remarkable and unexpected manner that I still marvel to this day, reliving the circumstances over and over in my heart and mind in order to glean one more bit of wisdom or guidance. Whenever I'm discouraged, I go back and read the dog-eared pages of my journal from this time, seeking the comfort and reassurance they always bring.

That night I lay awake in bed next to my wife in our small bedroom in the cabin on the Omineca River. She was sound asleep as I cradled her head with my left arm. Our unzipped sleeping bags, which we used as blankets, covered us as I peered around the cozy log room. My jeans hung over a ladder-back chair in the corner, my boots upright alongside it.

Then it struck me that the room wasn't dark, though it was not yet morning;

I could see everything clearly. No sooner had this thought occurred to me than I felt a terrific force pressing against my chest and face. The room filled with an ominous presence, thick and palpable. All around me countless dim shapes seemed to be struggling with one another, all possessed by some malign purpose. Somehow I knew they hated me, and that knowledge caused such terror in me that I was unable to move. I tried calling out, but I couldn't make a sound. Panic swept over me. Making one last desperate attempt I cried out, "In the name of Jesus Christ, deliver me."

Immediately light entered the room from the ceiling, flooding the room with a soft, warm, amber glow. The malignant shapes fled, and the crushing pressure on my chest subsided. I was even able to sit upright, but despite all that was happening, my wife still slept peacefully under the covers.

Before I could contemplate my deliverance, a figure descended in a column of light, and though he never spoke aloud, I knew him to be Moses, the prophet and lawgiver of the Old Testament. He stopped a few feet above the floor but remained close enough to me—just a few feet away—so I could easily examine his appearance. He had the look of a man between sixty and seventy years old, with white shoulder-length hair and a thin white beard. He wore a plain white robe with no additional adornment, at least none that I could see. It never occurred to me to pinch myself to see if I was dreaming; on the contrary, I felt such clarity and focus that it was as if my whole being had quickened to absorb the experience. Comfort enveloped me. Joy flooded my soul.

I had been raised in the church. I had attended Sunday school and catechism classes and had read Scripture all of my adult life. I had heard stories of angels appearing to men and women in ancient times. I knew about Moses himself hearing the voice of God from a burning bush. I knew that God had visited Abraham in his tent in Mamre and that Jacob had wrestled with a mysterious night visitor on the banks of the Jabbok. I was familiar with the story of Jesus on the Mount of Transfiguration when three of His closest friends and followers actually witnessed Him speaking to Moses and Elijah. But of course no one in his right mind ever expects anything like that to happen to *him,* especially not someone who was struggling spiritually. It made no sense at this point in my life. But at the time I knew nothing of what was to come.

The figure of Moses extended his right hand. In it was an off-white linen bag, cylindrical in shape, about twelve inches long and perhaps five inches in diameter, bound together in the middle by a drawstring tied in a simple bow. I reached out and took the small bundle and gently, reverently, began to untie it. I looked up briefly, but my visitor was no longer standing in the pillar of light. When I pulled the drawstring, its contents unfolded in my hands, revealing that the bag was actually a small waist apron, from which fell a simple robe-like garment of crude material, much like a flour sack.

Suddenly I was clothed in the robe through no effort or action of my own. My spirit must have slipped free of my physical body, because what I experienced from this point on took on an even more surreal quality. I felt both intense joy and unrestrained freedom of movement, as if I could travel anywhere I wanted. I found myself outside the cabin, where I was met by two radiant heavenly beings, one woman dressed in a long pale-blue robe and the other in pale green. They greeted me as if they had known me forever and proceeded to conduct me through a ceremony only slightly similar to rituals I had participated in during my religious training or read about in my studies.

The ceremony culminated, and before I could even savor the moment or ponder its significance, I found myself back in the little cabin in the Rocky Mountains, sitting straight up in bed next to my wife, who was still sound asleep. I jumped up, lit a candle, and went through the little cabin to see if anyone else was awake. I yearned to share the experience, but once I understood that no one would awaken for several hours, I forced myself to sit down and record every detail of the event in my journal while its trepidations and insurmountable joys were still fresh in my heart and mind.

For several days afterward I was high with the experience. My wife and our friends responded with amazement and understandable hesitation. As both my nature and my training dictated, I replayed the event repeatedly in my mind. I took long walks alone in the breathtaking landscape and sat for hours on the banks of the Omineca, trying to extract every possible shred of understanding and insight from my experience. But despite my best efforts, the visitation—or whatever it was—remained largely a mystery.

The one thing that was crystal clear to me was that the event was ultimately positive and divine in nature. The boundless wellspring of love and beauty that emanated from the being I understood to be Moses, and from the two sisterly beings, was all the confirmation I needed.

It would take the better part of another decade before I would begin to understand why I had been visited by Moses, who, according to rabbinical tradition, received the precise letter sequence of the Torah on Mount Sinai directly from God. Still, I knew beyond certainty that I was not deluded or deceived, and to this day I have been guided by that first spiritual experience in ways that underscore its reality and importance.

In 1989, at the time of that visit, much of the technology that would eventually make some sense of these things didn't yet exist, but without that strange encounter I would never have been drawn to investigate the revelations that lay ahead.

Awakening Awareness

Virginia, 1990

After that momentous experience in the Canadian Rockies, I became immersed once again in the world of art and antique restoration and appraisal. This time around, however, I approached my trade from a different perspective. I took far more interest in ancient artifacts and texts and particularly objects that compacted and communicated information.

I had more dreams, vivid visions that seemed to foreshadow the future, but they were difficult to read. Events in the dreams seemed disconnected from the circumstances of my waking life. People I had never known and others I had not seen in years featured prominently, especially the woman who would become my wife after my first marriage came to a painful end, but of course I knew nothing of this at the time.

Some dreams took me backward through time to unfamiliar places and circumstances that, strangely, were populated by my ancestors. In all this time I sensed that something was being communicated to me, though the nature of that message eluded me. Over time, however, one by one, the events in my life fulfilled the peculiar twists and turns seen in my dreams.

During those years I went through several seismic shifts in my personal life and circumstances. Not only did this period mark my broken family, but I found myself severing other longtime relationships and establishing new ones, a process that reminded me to be circumspect in talking about my experiences, my dreams, and what I would call an awakened spiritual awareness.

I was in my early thirties, and even though starting another family may not have been the wisest move financially, the remarkable events to come would never have taken place without it and this book would never have been written. And though those days were certainly not without their struggles, they also made for some wonderful memories.

My new wife and I decided to move from McLean, where our business was located, to the Alleghany Highlands of Virginia, about four hours away. We opened workshops near the tiny village of Monterey and transported restoration work from the Washington, DC, area back and forth every two or three weeks. The inconvenience was a small price to pay for the privilege of living in the most beautiful and least populated region east of the Mississippi. There, on long walks in the mountains and meadows that surrounded our small, sturdy brick home, I found the peace and solitude I craved after my experiences in the Canadian Rockies. I had resolved to take a far more open and reflective attitude in prayer than had previously been my inclination. I stopped pleading with God to answer all my questions, trying instead to open all my senses to Him and wait for Him to speak in His good time.

And He did.

Waiting for God to Speak

By the midnineties I was the father of six sons, with a girl finally on the way. My wife and I were homeschooling the three youngest boys, and she wanted to introduce them to various languages. Among those they attempted were some Native American dialects, particularly the Iroquois family.

While researching instructional material, my wife corresponded with the wife of Jake Thomas, hereditary chief of the Cayuga tribe at the Six Nations Reserve near Hamilton, Ontario. When she discovered that Chief Thomas was planning for the first time in history to make an English-language presentation of the *Gayanashagowa* ("Great Law of Peace"), the oral constitution that established and bound the Iroquois Confederacy together, she announced our next homeschooling field trip.

In early September 1996, with Hurricane Fran on our tail, we packed the kids and our camping gear into the van and headed five hundred miles north. We spent the next ten days at a rain-soaked campground just a few miles from the Jake Thomas Learning Centre. I'm pretty sure my boys learned a few things of value. I know I did. I was exposed for the first time to the Great Law, which was communicated from one generation to the next for hundreds of years using an object that looks to most people like nothing more than a beaded sash or wampum belt. It is much more than that, however. Conceived by the Great Peacemaker, Dekanawidah, and his spokesman, Hiawatha, the sash contains the 117 articles of the Great Law throughout Six Nations history.

In several private conversations with Chief Thomas, I asked about the encryption method employed on the beaded sash. Although from a distance the sash appeared to contain simple linear hieroglyphs, it was in fact a much more complex recording system that required many years of training to fully master.

I was fascinated by the use of symbolic, numeric, and chromatic elements to compact so much sacred history that it took ten days to unravel the information in an oral presentation: from the creation of the world by the Creator God, sometimes referred to in English as the Prophet of Peace, to organizational and governing issues that may have influenced the framers of the Constitution of the United States.

INTO THE MATRIX

I know this sounds mysterious, but I strongly believe that step by step I was being led by an unseen hand. One after another, new pieces of information showed up that broadened my understanding of the various ways different cultures communicated important information, often in coded form. Because of my experience in the Canadian Rockies, my radar was particularly tuned for any news, research, or other information related to ancient scrolls, especially if it related to the Torah and the Hebrew

Scriptures of the ancient Jews. I read the Bible voraciously. I even familiarized myself with Hebrew.

In 1997, my wife and I and our four youngest children moved to Martha's Vineyard, an island off the coast of Massachusetts. We had recently sold our business in Virginia, and I had signed a noncompete agreement that prohibited me from plying my trade in the Washington area for a while. We had discovered the Vineyard's charm quite by accident while exploring coastal New England in a small motor home. For the first time in my adult life I was no longer running a high-pressure business that required me to keep an endless stream of appointments with a demanding clientele.

Our first summer in Martha's Vineyard was spent enjoying the kicked-back lifestyle I had hoped for: gorgeous beaches, lobster diving, funky little cafés, and mobs of colorful people. When September rolled around and the crowds of tourists thinned, we rented a nice home up-island in Chilmark on the North Road, just a mile from the postcard-perfect Menemsha Harbor. It was an unhurried time, a chance to sleep in, and an ideal opportunity to make friends and enjoy guests who'd come to visit. It was also highly conducive to reading.

I continued my private research on ancient ceremonial objects, the types used in ancient and aboriginal ceremonies and rituals throughout the world, such as coronations, marriages, and initiations. Interestingly enough, many of these ceremonial objects ended up being brought to Martha's Vineyard, Nantucket, and other New England coastal towns by eighteenth- and nineteenth-century American sailors who collected them during their travels.

Once our Vineyard neighbors learned of my background and sought my opinion, I noticed the more I encountered such items from widely disparate lands and cultures, the more my research seemed to dovetail with an even more ancient source.

I spent much of that winter at Martha's Vineyard trying to make sense of some obscure academic articles. A handful of eminent scientists—mostly mathematicians, engineers, and physicists employing ever-expanding computer technologies—had observed perplexing anomalies, or oddities, in the composition and arrangement of the oldest Hebrew texts. It seemed clear to me that most of these scientists, hailing as they did from different institutions around the world, weren't comparing notes. I connected their discoveries as I followed the trail of ancient ceremonial devices and their tendency to use matrix-based data compaction similar to what I had already observed in the Iroquois Gayanashagowa.

Over and over again I found linkages and pointers leading back to the Hebrews and especially the Hebrew alphabet. The most curious connection, perhaps, was the fact that some Hebrew scholars as far back as the Middle Ages insisted that vast amounts of sacred information were somehow interwoven into the Torah, which of course predated any of the other systems I'd encountered. And given the fact that each of the twenty-two letters of the Hebrew alphabet expressed not only a phonetic sound but also a hieroglyphic meaning as well as a numeric equivalent, it would be the perfect alphabet to employ for matrix-based data compaction. Throughout much of ancient history, most writing was done on scrolls, which usually had writing on one surface and were attached to a rod at each end, allowing users to roll and unroll the document.

Then, between the fifth and tenth centuries AD, a group of Jewish scholars and scribes—working primarily in Tiberias on the western shore of the Sea of Galilee—devoted themselves to a task they believed of supreme importance not only for the Jewish people but also for all of humanity. These highly skilled scribes are generally referred to as the Masoretes, an abbreviation of the Hebrew term *ba'alei hamasorah* ("tradition keepers"). Modern biblical scholarship tells us the Masoretes not only employed strict protocols for copying the Hebrew Bible as we now know it but, in order to do so, spent generations collecting and preserving what they understood to be the most accurate biblical texts, which formed the foundation for their efforts.

The Masoretes developed exhaustive guides for pronunciation, grammar, and the ritual chanting of Scripture in order to standardize the way it was read and heard. These aids were achieved by meticulously positioning small diacritical marks around the letters of the text, with explanatory notes and possible variant readings inserted in the margins. But what separates the Masoretic tradition from nearly every other practice of textual transmission is its seemingly fanatical insistence that both the letter count and sequence of specific biblical manuscripts not be altered by so much as one letter.

All this was performed under the assumption that there was divine power contained in the precise placement of the letters in the text. For example, one famous interpreter of the Torah cautioned the scribes, "Be careful with your task, for it is sacred work; if you add or subtract even a single letter, [it is as if] you have destroyed the entire world!"[1]

Yes, they took their work that seriously!

The meticulous care taken by the Masoretes in precisely safeguarding the integrity of the Hebrew text also sprang from an ancient belief that the Torah was originally dictated to Moses by God, letter for letter. One Midrash, or ancient commentary, goes so far as to offer these details:

> Before his death, Moses wrote 13 Torah Scrolls. Twelve of these were
> distributed to each of the 12 Tribes. The 13th was placed in the Ark of the
> Covenant (with the Tablets). If anyone would come and attempt to rewrite
> or falsify the Torah, the one in the Ark would "testify" against him. (Like-
> wise, if he had access to the scroll in the Ark and tried to falsify it, the
> distributed copies would "testify" against him.)[2]

When I first learned of this claim, I was not surprised. After all, the practice of keeping a proof document for wills, deeds, royal edicts, genealogies, laws, and sacred manuscripts in a safe location was well established throughout the ancient world. At least one copy usually was held out of public circulation so authorities could use it to settle disputes or clear up any confusion that might arise. The most important documents were secured at a royal court or in temple archives.

This practice continues today in courthouses all over the world, and I've spent much of my career comparing historical objects to the stories that have been passed down with them, sometimes verifying and sometimes debunking those narratives based on forensic examination and reliable documentation.

Still, the more I learned about the Masoretes (and their predecessors among

Jewish scribes) and their meticulous work, the more impressed and excited I became, because in order to verify some of my hunches and research, I needed access to the most historically reliable version of the Scriptures.

A THOUSAND-YEAR-OLD BOOK

I had learned sometime earlier that the Leningrad Codex, so-called because it had long been kept in the National Library of Russia in Saint Petersburg (Leningrad) from 1924 to 1991, was the oldest complete text of the Hebrew Scriptures, or *Tanakh*,[3] which includes the Torah (the five books of Moses), the *Nevi'im* ("Prophets"), and the *Ketuvim* ("Writings")—what many call the Old Testament.

The codex, which looks and functions much like a modern book with multiple leaves bound on one side and writing on both sides of a leaf (each of which is referred to as a page), began to gain popularity in the Roman Empire during the first century AD, around the same time that parchment began to replace papyrus as the common writing surface. Early Christian writers preferred this structural design over scrolls, and by the Middle Ages the codex had become the format of choice for recording and preserving important and sacred writings throughout the Middle East and the Western world. (One notable exception is the *Sefer Torah* scroll, used for Torah readings in synagogues, which is produced according to stringent protocols and stored in a specially constructed cabinet.)

The Leningrad Codex, written on parchment and bound in leather, was in extraordinarily pristine condition after a millennium. The text of the codex contains the Hebrew letters that comprised the original text, along with tiny notations added by scribes to help with pronunciation and ritual chanting. To this day the Leningrad Codex is considered the oldest and most accurate complete example of the Masoretic text, which is the authoritative source text for nearly all translations of the Hebrew Scriptures, including *Biblia Hebraica* (1937) and *Biblia Hebraica Stuttgartensia* (1977). Other more recent translations, familiar to Christians worldwide, include the New International Version (NIV), the New Living Translation (NLT), the English Standard Version (ESV), and most other contemporary versions of the Bible.

According to generally accepted scholarship, the Leningrad Codex was created in Cairo, Egypt, around AD 1010 by Shemu'el ben Ya'aqov ("Samuel, son of Jacob"). It was apparently copied from manuscripts written in the city of Tiberias on the western shore of the Sea of Galilee by the famous scribe Aaron ben Moses ben Asher, sometime before his death in AD 960.

Its whereabouts for the more than eight hundred years that followed are a complete mystery. However, in the 1830s, Abraham Firkovich, a Crimean Karaite collector, agreed to include the codex in a large collection of rare documents offered for sale to what was then called the Imperial Public Library in Saint Petersburg for twenty-five thousand silver rubles. How or when Firkovich obtained the Leningrad Codex is unknown, but his colorful life and exploits have been the subject of much speculation by contemporary historians due to his acquisition of the finest early biblical manuscript collection. This achievement is ascribed to the fact that Firkovich was the first skilled collector of the nineteenth century to cherry-pick many of the best European and Middle Eastern synagogues, private collections, and *genizahs*[4] (storage areas for worn copies of the Hebrew Scriptures) in an apparent attempt to obtain relief and privileges for the Karaite Jews in the Russian Empire (amassing a sizable fortune for himself along the way). Thankfully, much of the fruit of his efforts (including the Leningrad Codex) is currently housed and protected at the National Library of Russia in Saint Petersburg.

During the last century the importance of the Leningrad Codex has grown due to the journey taken by an even older but incomplete codex: the "crown" of Aleppo. What scholars call the Aleppo Codex is a manuscript around which swirls so much intrigue, skulduggery, extortion, and calculated disinformation that efforts to uncover its history have taxed some of the best investigative journalists.

The Aleppo Codex was created in AD 920 by the scribe Shlomo ben Buya'a in Israel. About a hundred years after its production in the middle of the tenth century, the Aleppo Codex was purchased by Karaite Jews in Jerusalem and then promptly stolen by knights of the First Crusade who held it until Karaite Jews in Cairo, Egypt, paid a fortune for its ransom. It was then brought to Old Cairo, where it stayed for nearly three hundred years.

Later it was taken to the Central Synagogue in Aleppo, Syria, and placed in a special cabinet in an underground grotto that according to tradition was the cave of

Elijah. There it remained for 572 years, the pride of the faithful Jews of Aleppo, who guarded and protected it day and night.

Then, in December 1947, when the United Nations passed the historic vote to partition Palestine, the synagogue was attacked, ransacked, and set ablaze in an eruption of anti-Jewish violence. Although a story circulated that the Aleppo Codex had been consumed in the fire, ten years later it was smuggled into Israel. However, at some point in its journey from the Aleppo synagogue to Israel's Ben-Zvi Institute, 196 of the Aleppo Codex's 500 pages—nearly the entire Torah section—went missing.[5]

This meant that by the time I was born in 1960, the Leningrad Codex had replaced the Aleppo Codex as the oldest known complete copy of the Hebrew Tanakh.

HIDDEN TREASURES

In the course of my reading and research I found an article about a devoted group of specialists associated with the Ancient Biblical Manuscript Center based in Claremont, California.[6] That group had traveled to Saint Petersburg and taken high-quality photographs—for the first time in history—of the 966 pages of the famous Leningrad Codex and its 16 pages of the decorative geometric patterns that illuminate the text.[7] These facsimile photos had been published in a high-quality hardcover scholar's edition.

I wanted desperately to own a copy—until I saw the price: fifteen hundred dollars. To my amazement, however, I learned that I could request a copy of the codex through the interlibrary loan system.

So, after filling out my request at our small library at Martha's Vineyard, I waited expectantly for the arrival of the facsimile of the Leningrad Codex.

The Chamberlain Key

Massachusetts, 1998

It's difficult to describe what I felt when I first picked up that heavy facsimile of the Leningrad Codex at the library and took it back to our home off Menemsha Harbor. The connection between my adventure in the Canadian Rockies, my dreams, the journey my life had taken, and the events that led to that volume's publication all seemed surreal yet too strong to be seen as coincidence.

Though difficult to put into words, I had the strongest intuitive sense I would find some answers in this huge book of nearly eleven hundred pages.

At the time of my strange dream encounter with Moses in British Columbia, the Berlin Wall had not fallen and the Soviet Union strictly limited access to the Leningrad Codex. Western scholars knew about the codex, but few had ever seen it, let alone studied it. However, all that had changed during the years since my 1989 trip to the Canadian Rockies and when the first facsimile edition of the Leningrad Codex was published in 1998.[1]

That evening I waited until my children finished story time and trudged off to bed before I pulled out the hefty volume. A gale swelled outside, causing the windows and doors of the house to sigh and tremble as I opened the codex, marveling at line after line of beautiful black calligraphy that made up the Hebrew words, phrases, and sentences I had been learning to read for the past several years. I placed the Leningrad Codex on the carpet in the middle of the living room, pulled the floor lamp away from the wall, and adjusted the shade to position the light directly on the volume's pages.

Figure 4.A. The Leningrad Codex, Facsimile Edition.

I would soon know if I had been connecting the right dots or had been deceived by dreams and premonitions. I would either watch a thousand puzzle pieces come together into an unmistakable picture or see them scatter into a hopeless jumble. I knelt alone on my living room floor that winter night on a tiny island off the coast of Massachusetts and opened the book.

I quickly turned to a few verses in the first book of the Bible. For nearly a decade I had scoured the Bible in an effort to understand what I was supposed to do in the wake of my experience in the Canadian Rockies. Over time my search had focused more and more on the first book in the Bible: Genesis. More specifically, I found myself drawn to a single chapter—Genesis 30—and in particular to a short passage halfway through that chapter. I had settled on these verses because the story there had a puzzling similarity to my own family.

By the time we'd moved to Martha's Vineyard, my family consisted of my wife, six sons, and a daughter. The children were born in that order—first the six boys, followed by a girl—so when I saw this in one of my many readings of the story of the patriarch Jacob and his wives, Leah and Rachel, I was intrigued:

> And Leah said, God hath endued me with a good dowry; now will my husband dwell with me, because I have born him six sons: and she called his name Zebulun. And afterwards she bare a daughter, and called her name Dinah.
>
> And God remembered Rachel, and God hearkened to her, and opened her womb. And she conceived, and bare a son; and said, God hath taken away my reproach. (Genesis 30:20–23, KJV)

If you remember the story, those verses tell the straightforward tale of Jacob's two wives—the sisters Leah and Rachel—and how Leah gave birth to seven children while Rachel remained childless until the birth of Joseph. It always struck me as a curious coincidence that my parents' seven children *and* my own children followed the same pattern—six sons and a daughter—as that mentioned in Genesis 30:20–21. Until, that is, I obtained the Leningrad Codex and was able to scrutinize the verses more closely in the precise Hebrew text.

It was then I knew there might be more than mere coincidence at work in those odd parallels between Jacob's family and mine. I used the eraser end of a pencil to carefully count out some patterns in those verses in Genesis. I knew how to spell my name in Hebrew, and I used the exact nine-letter spelling that appears in the Hebrew translation of the New Testament found in Paul's letters to Timothy. Those nine Hebrew letters look like this: טימותיאוס.

I started at the first letter *T* or ט (*tet* in Hebrew) I found, then went on until I found an *I* or י (*yod* in Hebrew), noting there were exactly sixteen characters between them. Growing both more excited and nervous, I counted forward sixteen more Hebrew letters in the text and found the *m* or מ (*mem* in Hebrew). With my heart racing, I kept counting.

By the time I finished poring over the Leningrad Codex facsimile volume, I was trembling . . . and weeping like a child. I closed the expensive library book to protect its pages from my tears, set it aside, and lay down on the carpeted floor in an effort to control my emotions. I had found something that confirmed my suspicions. There, encrypted subtly in the Hebrew text, was my complete name.

I can understand if you think I had now drifted to the lunatic fringe; believe me, I have wondered that too. But I could not deny what my eyes were seeing.

I describe this as the moment I found the chamberlain key. In days long past the chamberlain was the official in a royal household who held the key, on behalf of the king, that gave access to the most private and secret areas of the castle or palace. He opened doors no one else could. I, too, had received a key to unlock a mysterious secret . . . from the King.

While the winter storm howled outside, my wife and children were safe and warm in their beds. And I, too, made some peace with storms of questions I'd had for years about my perplexing dreams. The long journey now had some glimmer of meaning. But what did this strange clue of my name really mean? How could I possibly know with greater certainty that what I had seen was true?

I sensed that even if I had made it to the foot of the mountain, I still had a long, hard climb to reach the peak.

I wiped the tears from my eyes and looked at the pencil I still held in my hand, the one I had used as a counter. I tried to flip the pencil into a mason jar sitting on the coffee table, but it pinged against the glass, rolled off the table, and disappeared under the sofa. I chuckled. It was high time I got a computer.

So the next stage of my journey began.

ENCRYPTIONS IN THE TEXT

My discovery, although an important milestone and very meaningful to me, set off many more years of personal doubt, searching, and investigation. By my nature and profession, I am a person who takes the need to verify truth most seriously.

During the years after my experience in the Canadian Rockies, I had combed through numerous academic articles, many of which had surfaced as a result of a paper by Dr. Eliyahu Rips and his associates, Doron Witztum and Yoav Rosenberg, that appeared in a 1994 issue of *Statistical Science.* It was titled "Equidistant Letter Sequences in the Book of Genesis."[2] Dr. Rips is one of the world's leading experts on an aspect of mathematics called geometric group theory. However, encryption using equidistant letter skips (EDLS) had been discovered as early as the thirteenth century by the Spanish rabbi Bachya ben Asher.

In their scholarly, peer-reviewed paper, Rips and the others concluded that the names of many famous rabbis were encrypted in the Masoretic text of the Hebrew Bible in close proximity to biographical information regarding those rabbis far more frequently than could be attributed to chance.

Later, the same conclusion was reached independently by Harold Gans, senior cryptologic mathematician for the US National Security Agency, who replicated their findings using his own computer program and achieved even greater statistical results.

This idea that the Hebrew text contained more than the information presented on the surface was not new. In fact, one of history's most acclaimed Torah scholars, Elijah ben Shlomo Zalman Kremer (also known as the Vilna *Gaon,* which means "genius from Vilna"), wrote the following in the eighteenth century:

And the rule is that whatever was, is and will be to eternity is all included in the Torah from "In the beginning" to "in the sight of all Israel." And not just the generalizations, but even the particulars of each and every species, and each specific person, and everything that will happen to him from the day he is born to his end, and all his detailed particulars. And similarly every species of animal and beast, and every living creature in the world and every herb and plant and mineral and all the detailed particulars of every species, and of the particulars of the species to eternity, and what will happen to them and their roots.[3]

Really? This is an amazing claim that, if true, relates to everyone—you and me included!

But the contemporary interest in the possibility of concealed messages in the Hebrew text might have faded into obscurity were it not for the publication of several popular books in the nineties. Michael Drosnin, an American journalist, created a publishing phenomenon with his international best seller *The Bible Code,* which drew from the work of Rips, Witztum, and Rosenberg. The book created a storm of controversy because of its spectacular claims about coming events.

Drosnin reminded me of countless people I've met in the course of my career who extract a few details from a given situation and enthusiastically tailor them to suit their own purposes. However, while such behavior in the case of heirlooms or antiques is relatively innocuous, I found *The Bible Code* appalling for many reasons.

For one thing, it treated the sophisticated concept of EDLS like a magic trick or a crystal ball to predict future events. That application of EDLS was invented by Drosnin; it had no foundation in the work of Rips or any other scientists and scholars working on the Hebrew text. Also, *The Bible Code*'s methodology was fatally flawed. Not a single discovery in the book can be said to have statistical significance based on a clear a priori condition. Each of Drosnin's "codes" could be attributed to chance.

To make matters worse, because of the flaws in *The Bible Code,* no one knows how many thousands or even millions of people dismissed Drosnin's claims out of hand. This Bible-code chaos led members of academia and the public at large, including many who placed little value on the Hebrew Scriptures anyway, to dismiss the whole process of EDLS as a fraud.

So although this sideshow provided some entertainment, I knew that my own path of careful research of the Hebrew text—if my hunches were correct—would lead to findings of much greater significance and meaning.

And in the meantime, I was also gathering related insights from my professional pursuits.

A RARE AND PRICELESS TREASURE

In 2003, on a rainy October day, I received a phone call from Cathy, a woman who operated a furniture-repair shop about a mile from my home. She had acquired some antique furniture, most of which looked ordinary, except for an early ladder-back chair that piqued her interest. She called it "very odd." I promised to come and take a look.

The sky had darkened ominously as I pulled up to Cathy's nineteenth-century building. Just as I stepped onto the covered front porch, a bolt of lightning struck nearby and a violent thunderclap rattled the storefront windows, accompanied by sudden sheets of rain. I knocked on the door and entered the shop.

"You must be living right. That was perfect timing," Cathy said.

I smiled. "Mostly I'm glad that lightning missed me, but it's nice to be dry too."

We shook hands and exchanged pleasantries about family and mutual friends. After catching up a little, I rubbed my hands together in my best impersonation of Fagin in *Oliver Twist*. "So what do you have for me today?"

"I'm not quite sure, but I figured you'd know."

Cathy lifted a chair from a wall peg and carried it over.

"Not bad." The piece was clearly an early Eastern Shore ladder-back, probably dating to sometime between 1790 and 1820. Ladder-backs, which required neither a lathe nor refined carving skills to create, were the most common country chair design in Virginia in the late eighteenth and early nineteenth centuries. "Definitely an early Shore piece. Look at the finials. I've seen those before, just like that. Just can't remember where exactly."

"How early is early?"

"Well, maybe as far back as the latter part of the eighteenth century, but it could be as late as 1830 or so. Craftsmen around here made these chairs pretty much the same way every time their whole lives. They didn't throw away their spoke shaves just because the century turned over. Where'd you find it?"

"Harley Parks owed me a hundred bucks. He got it along with a pile of stuff at Buck's Thursday night auction. Traded me a half dozen pieces to cover his bill. The rest of the load is only good for parts, but I wanted you to look at this."

"Well, I'm lookin'. It's got a great early oxide surface. Probably a buttermilk blood wash. Dollars to donuts there was once a split weave under all those calico rags on the seat."

"That's really why I called you. It's about what's under the calico."

The rain pummeled the big picture windows as Cathy knelt on the floor and carefully peeled back the cheap printed cotton fabric, one layer after another, each as worn and stained as the piece above it. There was nothing unusual about this. It was common practice at the time to freshen up a chair by placing a new piece of fabric over a worn seat covering. And it wasn't just about practicality. There were superstitions about discarding certain things, especially any material used by a parent or ancestor.

I nodded. "Yeah, seen that before. Kind of an Old World thing. Don't want to bore you with a lecture."

"You mean from England? Because that doesn't make sense. I've re-caned a gazillion chairs, Tim, and I've never seen this many old layers of fabric."

"No, not England. West Africa. People who lived on the Eastern Shore of Virginia when this chair was made were more likely to be West African than English. So did you get down to the split weave?"

"No. This is the last layer of cotton, I think, and I didn't go any further because I got this weird feeling about it. Yeah, from what I know, the West African explanation makes more sense, if by West African you mean African American."

"Yes. Thousands of years of culture and tradition didn't disappear because of American slavery; it just went underground. So is that what put the 'odd' in 'very odd' when you called?"

"Yeah, mostly. Do you think it's okay to see what's under this?"

"Why? What do you think you'll find?"

Her hand trembled slightly. "I took a peek at the edge and I saw some funny stitching. Symbols, maybe. I heard about the thing that was taken from the White House, the flag or whatever it was. How did you know where to find it? How did you track it down?"

Cathy's question referred to a donation I had arranged to the US Naval Academy Museum.

"You're talking about the Presidential Seal Pennant. It wasn't a flag, really."

"Steve Drummond saw it in your gallery before it went to the museum. He said it was beautiful, all hand-stitched silk on both sides. He said it was taken from the White House in the seventies or something, and you got it back for them."

"First of all, I prefer 'misplaced' instead of 'taken,' especially in a situation like that, where the trail usually leads to a retired congressman, senator, or presidential aide. I'd never get anywhere with them if I started off talking about a possible theft. I'm not the police anyway, and as far as my job goes, it doesn't matter how they came to possess it; it only matters that they do. But yes, it was gorgeous, in wonderful condition, and the only one of its type. But what does that have to do with this chair? Do you think Harley stole it?"

"No, not at all. He definitely bought it at the auction. I'm thinking about something Kelly Davis said you mentioned at the seminar you gave for the hospital benefit. You talked about certain traditions having to do with early textiles and something about symbols or emblems of state, that sort of thing."

"Oh, okay. I think I see what you're getting at."

"I did learn a little about where this chair came from, I mean, what family. A young man who needed money brought the stuff to the auction. You know Buck pays cash right on the spot."

"Go on." This was interesting, no doubt about it. Cathy was not the type to get easily carried away, so I took her feelings and hunches seriously.

"Well, my understanding was that this chair and the other things that came along with it had been found in an old house, not much more than a shack, where this kid's grandmother once lived, and that property was a part of the old Taylor land grant."

"Uh-huh." I knew the area well. When I first came to the Shore, I had purchased four old buildings on the Taylor land grant. They're often called dependences, a polite Southern term for the humble dwellings on a plantation where sharecroppers, former slaves, and descendants of slaves lived after emancipation. But they had been slave quarters. The little structures were at least 250 years old, and based on the artifacts I discovered in, around, and under them, I knew they had been lived in right up to the 1950s.

"Cathy, if it was a shack on the Taylor place and this chair came out of it recently, then I'm pretty certain I know which place it was. There was only one left; I salvaged all the others four or five years ago."

Cathy nodded, then set the chair upside down on the floor and began carefully removing the tacks underneath the seat rails. In just a few minutes the last outer covering fell to the floor. She set the chair upright, and my suspicions were confirmed. I was looking at what most people call a crazy-quilt pattern, but it was obviously much older than any late nineteenth-century Anglo American example and was completely composed of what appeared to be eighteenth-century woolens.

"That's the weirdest scrap of crazy quilt I've ever seen," Cathy said. "And look at this." She turned the chair upside down again. "I was wondering what these were. This covering isn't tacked to the chair; it's just tied on at the corners, and there's three sets of them."

Working together, we carefully untied the first covering. Underneath it was an even more unusual piece of needlework, also made from what appeared to be eighteenth-century wool. There were nine symbols arranged on a grid pattern: three linear symbols each composed of three lines, three figurative symbols (a spider, spider web, and cosmogram), and three twelve-pointed stars.

"What is this?" Cathy asked. "I'm a quilter and a needleworker, and I've never seen anything like it."

"It's definitely African American, no doubt in my mind. And not just the needlework, but the chair itself looks like a Chandler or a piece made in the same tradition. There's one in the old debtor's prison," I said, referring to a familiar historic landmark in Accomack County, just north of us.

There was still one more layer to examine. "Let's untie this one and have a look at the one on the bottom." My senses were tingling. This was shaping up to be something extraordinary.

Cathy nodded and slowly removed the covering, revealing the last piece of needlework.

"Take a look at that," I said. "Oh my gosh. This thing looks complete. And pristine. If it's okay with you, I'd like to spend some time with this. I have some suspicions about what this thing actually is—and it's a bit complicated."

Cathy agreed to let me spend the necessary time on it, and a year later I presided over a meeting at the National Geographic Society in Washington, DC, focused on this remarkable African American artifact. From the earliest days of slavery in Vir-

ginia, the majority West African population in the pre- and postcolonial period operated their own underground system for communicating between plantations. The
preservation of West African cultural traditions was most pronounced on the Del-
marva Peninsula, where many slaves were transported directly from West Africa to
the Chesapeake region without a multigenerational interlude in the Caribbean. Virginia's Eastern Shore—with its nearly endless number of small islands, secluded
necks, and marsh areas—also served as a haven, however precarious, for escaped
slaves who interacted via a well-established underground with enslaved West Afri-
cans as well as with the many freed blacks living on the northern end of the
peninsula.[4]

Cathy's chair was not only a physical memorial to this separate nation hidden
from Anglo American society but, I determined, a complex mnemonic device for the
transmission of information across miles, cultures, and generations[5]—a secret language used for ceremonial purposes. I identified the chair as one of the most remarkably well-preserved representations of West African cultural, religious, and
cosmological traditions ever to survive the trauma of the transatlantic slave trade, an
important example of the way slaves tried to preserve and pass on their memories
and traditions.

I presented my research to members of the staff and discussed the possibilities
for the final disposition of that African American secret-society chair. Sometime later
I arranged for the donation of this artifact to the new United States National Slavery
Museum slated for construction in Fredericksburg, Virginia.[6]

The ladder-back chair served to increase my awareness of just how many secrets
are still out there waiting to be discovered. It also roused my interest in the technique
of using two-dimensional arrays as a way of compacting and transmitting information, particularly when the information was considered sacred.

I realized that arranging various symbols on a two-dimensional grid allowed for
each one to act as a data bit that could occupy three positions in space: vertical, horizontal, and diagonal. This system of encryption bore a striking similarity to modern
universal product codes and quick-response codes, which use numeric, alpha-
numeric, binary, and symbolic characters to compact product information on a small

two-dimensional surface like a bar code or a QR code. Both historical and modern systems are undecipherable to the casual observer; they require either specialized training or a scanning device to extract the encoded information.

In this way an old chair contributed to the major discovery that still lay in my future, concealed in the ancient text of the Hebrew Torah.

A Passionate Search

As the years passed, like any father responsible for supporting a large family, I spent most of my waking hours working to make all the ends meet. But when I had spare hours, I continued to seek ways to verify my developing theories about the apparent complexity of the ancient Hebrew text. As computer technology—both hardware and software—developed, I found some programs that aided my analysis.

When I knocked on the doors of scientists, language specialists, museum curators, private researchers, and highly placed individuals in the intelligence community in my quest to understand the significance of my discoveries, somewhat surprisingly (even to me), I found support for the credibility of Rips, Witztum, and Rosenberg's work. But you'd never know that if your primary exposure to that research was based on the widespread discrediting of the book *The Bible Code*.

Ultimately, *The Bible Code* may have been misleading and silly, but as much as I was dismayed by the book and nearly all of its claims, I could not dismiss the evidence I had discovered of precognitive messages interwoven with the lines and letters of the Hebrew text. I couldn't come close to comprehending the breadth and depth of it all, but the outlines of the concepts were becoming progressively more clear.

And then some others got involved . . .

Part II

UNDER SCRUTINY

A Door Opens

Virginia, 2013

He walked into my Eastern Shore Virginia gallery wearing a Donegal tweed hat. Thin and spry, with watery blue eyes and hair tucked neatly under his hat, he looked like he might be in his late seventies. I sat at the gallery's command center, a high L-shaped counter from which I could see the entire room without immediately being noticed by someone coming in the front door. It was a Saturday. My staff was off for the weekend, so I had no one to run interference for me or he would have been politely intercepted and offered assistance. I greeted him myself without wanting to be intrusive. "If there's any way I can help you, please let me know."

"It just so happens we may be able to help each other," he replied. His voice possessed an Old World quality, conveying both confidence and panache.

Definitely selling something, I decided.

He gestured to the big Chippendale wing chair next to my counter reserved for cozy conversations with good clients and friends. "Okay if I sit down here and take a load off these old knees?" He seated himself without waiting for an answer.

I swung around in my high-back swivel chair to face him as he thrust his hand in my direction. "My name is Dan Murphy, and I think we have several mutual acquaintances from the old country."

I shook his hand. I couldn't help but like his style. Whatever he was selling, I figured he believed in it. Since it was a slow, dreary March day, I decided to go along for the ride. "I don't have many acquaintances back in Ireland, Mr. Murphy, so you may have me confused with someone else."

"Oh no, I know who you are, Mr. Smith. And the old country to which I refer is Washington, DC. Can I call you Tim, or do you prefer Timothy?"

I grinned. "You can call me anything but Timmy. Only my mother calls me that."

"Timothy, then. Are you *the* Timothy in Timothy Smith and Sons, or are you one of the sons?"

"I'm *the* Timothy," I said. "I have sons, but none of them is named Timothy." This guy was right out of a Humphrey Bogart movie. I liked him more by the second.

"That's right, then. Your father is E. Jay Smith. Your grandfather was Clarence Smith. And you've got six sons, if I'm not mistaken."

Who *was* this guy? I wondered if I should recognize his name. "Actually, it's six sons and a daughter. And how do you know about my father?"

"I was a White House press correspondent in the Kennedy days. In fact, I was the only correspondent in the White House when word broke that JFK had been shot. Everyone else was in Dallas. Strangest day of my life. I think I met your father in McLean around then. He was working on something interesting."

Just then the front door opened and Michael walked in. He was my best fine-art conservationist, probably stopping by to pick up a well-earned check.

"Hey, Mike," I said. "You must have wrapped up your latest mission impossible. What do I owe you?"

"I can come back if you're busy." Michael knew that someone sitting in the big chair usually meant important and potentially profitable business for me.

I rose from my seat. "No, actually, why don't you take my seat and chat with Dan Murphy here while I head for the bathroom." I gave Michael a wink. "Compare notes with him for a minute. He's from inside the Loop."

I didn't walk down the hall to the bathroom but slipped into my office and shut the door. I had to satisfy my curiosity. A second later I was looking at an image of a younger Daniel Murphy in 1963. He was heavier in those days, but it was definitely the same man. So he really did know Jack and Bobby. A photo showed him on *Air Force One* with Lyndon Johnson. He was with the *Washington Post.* More photos. Schmoozing at parties. With his wife. Even a more recent shot of him with Edward Cardinal Egan. So he was who he said he was.

I strained to listen through the door to Dan's conversation with Michael. He said something about having once worked as an investigator for Lloyd's of London. Michael, always polite, responded by extolling the virtue of jobs that afforded opportunities to travel the world.

I returned to the gallery. "Thanks for entertaining Mr. Murphy for me, Mike. How about we catch up tonight at the Parsonage?"

Michael nodded at my reference to the pub next door and exchanged a few final pleasantries with Dan. He turned toward the door then, but not before shooting me a look that suggested I was in for a doozy of a conversation.

I settled back into my chair and asked Dan Murphy as delicately as possible to cut to the chase.

He took the hint and jumped right to it. "As I was telling your friend, after my days at the *Post,* I did some detective work with Lloyd's of London. I used to track down stolen property for them. I loved that kind of work, very exciting. My specialty was stolen jewelry."

"That *would* be fun. So is that why you came to see me? You're hunting some missing jewels, and you think I can help you?"

"No, no, nothing like that. But I did hear through the grapevine that you had discovered something rather interesting." He lowered his voice when he said this, though there was no one else in the room.

"I've found lots of interesting things. You're going to have to narrow it down a bit."

"I'm talking about something you found in the Bible. Something strange in the original Hebrew text."

I knew exactly what he was referring to, but I had good reasons for being cautious. On the few occasions I shared bits and pieces of my research with people, it led to questions I was either unable or unwilling to answer, and often the answers required far more background information than anyone had time for. I had been searching for answers for well over a decade for what I had found in the Hebrew text.

"I know you've discovered something," Dan continued, "and I know you're not the type to be easily impressed with an oddity or coincidence. The person I spoke to said you were stunned by what you found, and that's a strong word. Makes me wonder what could have made such a big impression."

I began to speak, but my guest wasn't finished. He leaned forward in that big wing chair. "I once got an interview with Jimmy Hoffa through sheer persistence."

I smiled. "Did Jimmy Hoffa tell you what you wanted to know?"

"No, but I talked to the man himself, which was more than anyone else in my office had been able to do. And I got a lot of mileage out of it."

"So what are you planning to do with whatever information I give you? You can't publish it."

"No, no, of course not. I would never do anything like that without your permission."

"I'd like to know more about why you're so interested in what I'm doing with the Hebrew Scriptures. Are you writing a book?"

The gallery door opened, ringing its polite little bell as two middle-aged couples entered and glanced around. I left Dan to greet the shoppers and offer what assistance I could. When the ladies in the party began to set aside a pile of potential purchases on the walnut tavern table I left clear for that very purpose, I let them know I'd be nearby if they needed me and walked back over to Dan. He hadn't budged from the comfy wing chair. He seemed to be thoroughly enjoying himself. I bent down and whispered in his ear.

"If you really want to know what I think on that subject, you're going to have to sign a nondisclosure agreement. And then we can meet someplace private. Right now I have business to attend to."

"That'll be fine. I'll sign whatever you want."

Even then he showed no intention of giving up his seat. His demeanor was that of someone who belonged right where he was as he offered helpful comments to my customers and regaled the two men with a story about how Lyndon Johnson kept trying to steal Dan's piece of pecan pie when he and the press were guests on *Air Force One*.

After half an hour the ladies had gathered nearly fourteen thousand dollars in purchases. I had the porcelain, silver, paintings, and nice Persian prayer rug rung up, packed, and loaded in the trunk of their Mercedes when Dan Murphy said his good-byes and went on his way.

A week after I first met Dan Murphy, the time had come for a follow-up meeting. After I steered my Chevy Silverado down the half-mile tree-lined lane to his seaside house, Dan's golden retriever, Cody, welcomed me enthusiastically in the circular drive. By the time Dan opened the front door, Cody had covered my Harris Tweed overcoat in dog hair. It was a foggy, dank afternoon on the Eastern Shore, so I was delighted to see a steady wisp of smoke rising from the chimney near the back of the expansive contemporary home.

"Don't mind Cody. He loves everybody." Dan invited me in and took my coat. "There's someone waiting in the den I want you to meet."

"Mr. Murphy, I don't want to be rude, but I wasn't expecting anyone else to be here today. I'm serious about the nondisclosure, and my attorney has prepared a copy for you to sign before we get started."

"Please call me Dan, and no worries at all. We'll just make a copy of that agreement for my friend, and he'll sign one as well. How about that?"

"Who exactly is your friend?"

"Relax. You two have a lot in common."

The log fire blazed beautifully in a massive native-stone fireplace that formed the centerpiece of a large book-lined den. Cody had followed us in and curled up on the worn leather sofa that faced the fire. As we entered the room, a heavyset man I judged to be in his late sixties rose from one of the two wide leather club chairs flanking the sofa. I set my briefcase on the massive cocktail table constructed from an old ship's hatch and withdrew a folder containing the nondisclosure agreement.

The man extended his hand, and I shook it.

"Robert Dallet. Nice to meet you. Dan has told me some very interesting things about you. I hope you don't mind my being here."

Dan took the nondisclosure agreement and disappeared into an adjoining office.

"Well, Dan and I just met the other day. So I'm curious what interesting things he might have said about me." I assumed Dan had researched me, as I had him. I also figured that Dan didn't want to give me time to do the same with Robert Dallet.

"Well, I'll be totally up front with you. I sort of pushed my way into this situation because I'm fascinated with something Stella Freeman—a mutual acquaintance of ours, I believe—told me about some research you've been doing related to the Hebrew Old Testament. You do know Stella, don't you?"

Before I could answer, Dan came back in the room with a fresh copy of the agreement in hand. He directed Robert and me to sit in the well-worn Ernest Hemingway chairs while he took a seat on the couch next to Cody. I waited while the two men signed the agreements and handed them to me. I wasn't opposed to sharing certain aspects of my discoveries under the right circumstances, but few people had the background or interest to properly understand my findings. Stella Freeman, to whom Robert had referred, was one of those people. A professor of religious iconography, she had her own collection of early native and aboriginal textiles, some of which I had secured for her. Stella had been in my gallery six months previously and had noticed on my computer monitor a two-dimensional array of Hebrew script. She politely inquired what I was up to. One thing led to another, and before long she was engrossed and requesting more and more information.

I told Robert I knew Stella well. "She's a good client and a lovely person. And yes, she and I have talked about my research. I gave her my perspective on the Leningrad Codex and the Masoretic Hebrew text in general and how its structure relates to other ancient communication systems. She collects early textiles and of course is aware of the encryption systems used in a lot of this stuff, so I didn't have to explain all that."

Dan nodded enthusiastically. "She was excited about the ingenious ways people from all over the world communicated in the past: drumbeats, signal fires, message runners, that sort of thing. But she was especially interested in coded military communications in ancient Greece and Rome. Maybe Egypt too. I can't remember, but she went on and on about it. She said you had an eye for the artifacts used in some of this communication."

"She said more than that," Robert said. "She said you could decipher some of this encrypted communication better than anyone she had ever met. She said you were using what you had learned in the old Hebrew text to work out the other systems."

"Well, maybe the West African ones. I found the greatest similarities in those examples, especially textiles. I think the concepts moved down from North Africa via trans-Saharan caravan routes perhaps as far back as 1000 BC. Things were pretty advanced in that part of the world right on up to the fourteenth century AD. There was a lot of interaction with the major Mediterranean powers as well, but I don't think the system was indigenous to West Africa. I think it originated with the Hebrews."

"Exactly what system are you talking about?" Robert asked.

Dan poured us something to drink and waited as I considered how to express this rather complex concept as simply and concisely as possible.

I accepted the glass from Dan and took a sip. "The system is one in which a two-dimensional array or grid is used to position letters, symbols, or images with the aim of compacting as much information as possible onto the smallest possible surface. Every element added to the system increases its efficiency."

"What elements?" Robert asked. "Do you mean three- or four-dimensional arrays?"

Dan cleared his throat. "You guys are talking above my pay grade, and you've completely confused Cody. I want to know what Mr. Smith has found in the Bible!"

"If that were the case, it would be over my head as well," I said, responding to Robert's question. "When I say other elements, I mean things like color or iconographic modifications, stuff like that. If the symbols or letters employed in the system have a known numerical equivalent, then that dramatically increases the efficiency, since you now have the ability to communicate in the universal language of mathematics."

"Like that movie," Dan said, snapping his fingers. "With what's-her-name—the one who listens for intelligent signals from outer space. *Connection* or something like that."

I smiled. "*Contact*. And it was Jodie Foster. Based on a book by Carl Sagan, the popular astronomer and an astrophysicist. And there are similarities between what I'm talking about and the concept Sagan portrayed in his book. Same basic idea."

Dan shook his head, but Robert was nodding and smiling. "Yeah, Stella said that you had definitely picked up signs of complex intelligent communication some-how interwoven into the Hebrew text of the Bible."

I shrugged. "Stella likes the word *interwoven* because of her love of antique textiles, but an astrophysicist might use a different word, like *encrypted*. Sagan spec-ulated that if mankind were ever to receive a signal from some nonearthly intelli-gence that the communication would begin with an unmistakable signal in the language of basic mathematics."

Dan's face lit up. "That was the contact in the movie—a loud, evenly spaced radio signal—but the math part came later, right? Prime numbers or something?"

"Yes and no. The audio pulse was also mathematic—the most basic math, in fact, the type of signal that scientists know can only come from an intelligent source. It's called equidistance, which means evenly spaced. Let's say the audio signals were pulsating at exactly five-second intervals; random noise in space doesn't do that, not ever. So it's the most basic way an intelligent being can get the attention of another intelligent being. If you were marooned on what you thought was an uninhabited island, and one morning you woke up and found ten evenly sized stones lined up on the beach exactly ten feet apart from each other, you might figure that someone else was on the island. If the same thing happened ten mornings in a row, you'd be sure of it."

Robert perched himself on the edge of his chair. "So what you're saying is that you've found signals in the Hebrew Old Testament as convincing as that?"

I took a long sip and stared into the fire. Despite the signed nondisclosure forms, I knew I was putting my personal and professional credibility on the line. I set the glass on the table.

"No, I'm going beyond that," I finally responded. "I want to be very clear about this: I'm saying that I've found perfect mathematical structures and signals in the

Leningrad Codex, the oldest complete copy of the Masoretic text of the Old Testament. These signals would be as scientifically and statistically convincing as if you woke up one morning on that uninhabited island and found thousands of perfectly spaced stones on the beach spelling out the message HELLO, DANIEL MURPHY. I HOPE YOU ARE FRIENDLY. I HAVE SOMETHING I WANT TO GIVE YOU. No matter how convinced you'd been up to that point that you were alone on the island, you'd be forced to admit that you were wrong."

The room fell silent. My companions stared at me as if waiting for me to break into laughter and pronounce it all a joke.

Dan broke the silence. "Are you saying the communication is from God?"

Robert jumped in before I could answer. "The Leningrad Codex was transcribed in the Middle Ages, I think. Is it possible that a clever scribe or rabbi encrypted the messages?"

I shook my head. "The messages are precognitive."

"You mean messages about the future?" Robert asked.

"No, I'm not talking about fortune-telling. When I say precognitive, I mean that the intelligence that originally designed or composed the precise letter sequence of the text knew things that were simply not known at the time the text was created, and thus must have been coming from a perspective of timelessness, or outside of time as we know it. Modern physicists are aware of the concept. So if it was a scribe or rabbi in the tenth century, somehow he stepped out of time and into eternity."

"So it could have been God," Dan said.

"Of course it could have been God," I said. "Jewish tradition—based on the words of the Torah, for example in Deuteronomy 31:24–26—says that God originally revealed to Moses the precise letter sequence of the Torah, and Moses wrote it on a lambskin scroll and had the Levites place the scroll in the ark of the covenant in the tabernacle. If you want to come up with another scenario, that's fine, but you'd be cutting it from whole cloth. Based on what I've found, it appears that the three-thousand-year-old explanation is the one that makes the most sense."

When he spoke, Dan's tone was more serious than anything I'd heard from him yet. "Timothy, if what you're saying is true—and by the way, I have a good friend who is an astrophysicist and the dean of engineering at a top Ivy League university — if what you're saying can be proven empirically, then it would be the most remarkable discovery of our age. I think you should make it public, let scholars evaluate it, and see if it passes muster. My astrophysicist friend is agnostic, as far as I know, and he has a great deal of experience with this precognitive thing you're talking about. He works with legions of other scientists from all over the world, and they could help you figure this out—unless, of course, you don't want anyone looking over your shoulder."

"Not at all," I said. "I'd be delighted to have someone looking over my shoulder. I've been gathering this information for more than fifteen years. And in some ways it has been a heavy burden to carry alone."

"Why have you kept it to yourself?" There was a note of genuine concern in Robert's voice. "What are you afraid of?"

"A picture is worth a thousand words," I answered.

The Key Code

Virginia, 2013

The time had come to step out on a limb. I opened my briefcase, pulled out my laptop, and turned it on. After a long wait (by today's standards, at least), I opened a computer program that contained the exact letter sequence of the Leningrad Codex with various functions that allowed for reconfiguring that sequence based on precise mathematical parameters. I gave Dan and Robert a quick tutorial on the software and showed them why it was impossible for me to have monkeyed with the search results. I even gave them the name of the Israeli company that published and sold the software, inviting them to obtain their own copies to dispel any suspicion that I might have tampered with the program.

After the tutorial, I took a notebook out of my briefcase, found the single sheet of paper I wanted, and placed it on the table.

"Can you guys figure out what this is?" I asked.

They both glanced at it for a moment and nodded.

"Here I have recorded detailed biographical information about one particular real-life modern family: *mine.*" I held up the sheet and turned it to face them. "Here's the full name of the husband, wife, six sons, and one daughter, complete with exact birthdates." I pointed farther down the page. "Here you've got the husband's father, his wife, his six sons and one daughter and all their birthdates. All this information can be checked in public records. It's just straightforward biographical detail, and all of it from the second half of the twentieth century."

"Two families with the same unusual configuration. That's quite a coincidence," Dan observed. Robert Dallet seemed to be concentrating, maybe trying to do the math in his head.

"I'll save you the effort," I offered. "The odds of a man having six sons and a daughter and then one of his sons also having six sons and a daughter is millions to one. But in and of itself that has no meaning. Like Dan said, it's just a coincidence."

I turned to the computer. "Robert, you asked why I've been keeping this to myself. I think what I'm about to show you will answer that question."

I typed in the Old Testament reference I wanted. "In some ways, this is where it started for me, though it took a long time for all the pieces to come together. But one day my funny little family coincidence—which came about only when my daughter was born in 1997, just before the first facsimile of the Leningrad Codex was published—led me to a specific biblical reference."

I pointed to the screen, where parallel portions of Genesis 30 were displayed. "See, here's the original Hebrew text on the right and the English translation on the left. Is there any mention in the book of Genesis of someone having six sons and then a daughter?"

Robert pointed. "I'm ahead of you on this one. That would be Jacob and Leah."

"Okay. So now let's isolate that particular verse. Give me two seconds. Okay, here it is in Hebrew. And you see the English over on the left."

English	Hebrew
[20] And Leah said, God has endowed me with a good dowry; now will my husband live with me, because I have born him six sons; and she called his name Zebulun.	[20] ותאמר לאה זבדני אלהים אתי זבד טוב הפעם יזבלני אישי כי ילדתי לו ששה בנים ותקרא את שמו זבלון
[21] And Afterwards she bore a daughter, and called her name Dinah.	[21] ואחר ילדה בת ותקרא את שמה דינה
[22] And God remembered Rachel, and God listened to her, and opened her womb.	[22] ויזכר אלהים את רחל וישמע אליה אלהים ויפתח את רחמה
[23] And she conceived, and bore a son; and said, God has taken away my reproach;	[23] ותהר ותלד בן ותאמר אסף אלהים את חרפתי

Figure 6.A. Genesis 30:20–23 in English and in Hebrew.

Dan watched attentively but said nothing. Robert spoke again.

"Okay, that's interesting. But how does that relate to this modern family?" He nodded at the page with my family information.

"Which of the six sons in the first family is the one who also had six sons and afterward a daughter?"

Dan pointed to the fourth son, Timothy—me. "That's you. Okay, we're with you so far. Go on."

"Does my name mean anything to either of you? Are you familiar with its origins?"

Robert shrugged slightly. "Isn't it a common Greek name, *Timotheus*? One of Paul's disciples in the New Testament?"

"Yes, that's right. The name also shows up in the second book of Maccabees[1]— *Timotheus* is some sort of Greek military commander[2]—but the name is believed to have ancient Ionian origins as far back as the eighth century BC. The name shows up all over the place in early Hebrew documents, and it's spelled exactly the same way in the Hebrew translation of the New Testament." I pulled up the Hebrew name database in the program and showed them what the spelling of the name would look like using Hebrew letters. "There it is, *Timotheus*. Nine letters long and phonetically straightforward." The English reads left to right; the Hebrew reads right to left.

Timotheus טימותיאוס

"Got it," Robert said.

"Do you read Hebrew?"

"I'm no Hebrew scholar, but I know the sounds of the letters, and with a good concordance and enough time, I can work out their meaning."

"Fair enough. So I imagine you're aware that each of the twenty-two letters in the Hebrew alphabet has a numerical equivalent."

"Yes, I am."

"Well, here's a quick math game for both of you." I pulled a loose leaf from my notebook. "Here's a sheet showing all the Hebrew letters and their numeric equivalents. See if you can work out the sum value of the letters that make up this nine-letter name."

They turned to the task with alacrity, while I took a few sips of my drink, enjoyed the fire, and scratched Cody's ears.

"Eleven hundred and two," Dan announced with an official flair.

Robert wrote the number in pencil on the sheet. "Agreed."

"Good. So we're still having fun here, right? What is the reduced sum of eleven hundred and two?"

Dan smiled. "Don't need an astrophysicist for that. It's four. One plus one plus zero plus two. Equals four."

"Right. Now in the Hebrew tradition everything is reduced to its simplest terms, its root, or the essence of its meaning. That's what symbols, glyphs, and iconography are all about—a simple symbol packed with meaning—and that's how biblical Hebrew words are composed and interpreted. I know this sounds arcane, but these details will help you better appreciate what I'm about to show you."

"Go ahead. I'm with you," Robert said. "I've studied a lot of this before. It's coming back to me. Also you've got that thing in Hebrew and Greek where nearly every name has a specific meaning, a phrase made up of its root elements. So that name, *Timotheus,* means 'honored of God' or 'God's honor' if you just put together the Greek root words." He laughed. "My Greek is better than my Hebrew."

"Yes, that's exactly right. And it turns out to be an important detail, because this name is what I call the key code that unlocks the hidden internal structure of the text. And just like a mechanical key, every little tooth, notch, and groove is necessary to release the lock. In fact, the first appearance of this word or name—this nine-letter sequence—takes place in the book of Genesis, in the Hebrew Torah."

"That name is definitely not in the Torah," Robert protested.

Dan had stepped over to the stone fireplace to add a couple of logs to the fire. Over his shoulder he said, "I get the feeling he's about to show us that it is."

"Yes, I am. But first I want to go back to our discussion about the movie

Contact and how astronomers and astrophysicists speculated that if humankind was to receive a signal from an intelligent entity from some other place or dimension in the universe, it would most likely arrive in the form of an equidistant pulse or signal."

Robert rubbed his chin. "But even if you could show that a signal in an ancient text was placed there, how could we know it was from somewhere unearthly? Wait," he said, interrupting himself. "Never mind. The signal would have to demonstrate precognitive attributes, like you were talking about."

"That's right, it would be nonlocal, as in not from time and space as we experience it, but from a realm beyond time—the place where the ancient Hebrews believed Yahweh dwelled. But this is the part an astrophysicist might really appreciate, though it's pretty basic. Pinpointing a location on the surface of the earth requires at least two reference points: longitude and latitude. Pinpointing a position in three-dimensional space requires at least three coordinates, which is the way a GPS works. But the only accurate way to pinpoint something in historical earth time is with precise *biographical* data points."

I picked up the page of family information from the table. "That's what this sheet is loaded with: names, birthdates, birth order, place of birth, spousal connections, and so on. With these data points, we can fix these people's locations in time. The more data points you have, the more precise the fix. Are you with me?"

Dan returned to his seat, nodding, as Robert answered, "Yes, no problem with that. But get back to this business of a key code, the name that isn't there but really is."

I stood and leaned over the computer. "Okay, then, just keep your eyes on this computer and watch. So the reduced sum of our key code is four, and the fourth son happens to be Timothy, who had six sons and then a daughter, just as his father did and just as Jacob did with Leah. And here on the screen are the four verses in Genesis—in English—that mention Leah and her six sons and one daughter. Now look at this. Here is our key code—*Timotheus*—all nine letters in perfect order inside those few verses, placed at an exact equidistance of sixteen." I pointed to each of the letters with the tip of my pen.

²⁰ ותאמר לאה זבדני אלהים אתי זבד טוב הפעם
יזבלני אישׁ כי ילדתי לו ששה בנים ותקרא
את שמו זבלון

²¹ ואחר ילדה בת ותקרא את שמה דינה

²² ויזכר אלהים את רחל וישמע אליה אלהים ויפתח
את רחמה

²³ ותהר ותלד בן ותאמר אסף אלהים את חרפתי

Figure 6.B. The nine-letter key code, *Timotheus,* at an
equidistant letter skip (EDLS) of sixteen.

"Now let's ask the computer program to realign this tiny section of text into a sixteen-column two-dimensional array. No tweaking here; it has to be sixteen columns because the equidistant placement of the letters on the key code was exactly sixteen." I realigned the text with a click of my laser mouse. "Robert, what do you see smack-dab in the middle of the array? Use those Hebrew skills."

Robert said nothing. He stood and stepped closer to the table, concentrating on the matrix in the middle of the glowing screen as if it were a crystal ball. Suddenly, Cody jumped off the couch, stared at Robert, and barked for the first time since I'd met him.

"Here, I can highlight it for you." I used my pencil to point out what I wanted them to see in a single vertical column of the Scripture passage.

"There it is in Hebrew: *Timotheus.*"

Dan was looking at Robert more than the computer screen. "Don't look so shocked, Bob. I mean, that makes sense, doesn't it? If the key code is in the text at an equal spacing of sixteen and you then divide the text into sixteen columns, it should line up like that, right?"

Robert spoke softly and deliberately. "Yes, I see that. And I know the odds of this would be billions, maybe trillions to one, especially since you called your shot in

ר ל א ה ז ב ד נ י

י ז ב ד ט ו ב ה פ

י א ש י כ י י ל

ה ב נ י ם ו ת ק ר

ב ל ו ז ו א ח ר י

ק ר א א ת ש מ ה ד

ר א ל ה י ס א ת ר

א ל י ה א ל ה י ם

ר ח מ ה ו ת ה ר ו

א מ ר א ס ף א ל ה

ת י ו ת ק ר א א ת

Figure 6.C. *Timotheus* in a single vertical column when the text is realigned based on the EDLS spacing of sixteen.

advance. But that's not what I'm staring at." He picked up the sheet with the biographical information, and with his forefinger he pointed to my wife's name. When he did that, I knew that Robert could read Hebrew better than he was letting on. "I see you have your wife's full maiden name on the sheet. It's a very unusual name and very beautiful." He turned to me and put his hand on my shoulder. "I get it now. And I understand your caution too."

Dan Murphy looked back and forth between the computer screen and the two of us. "All right, you two, don't make me think too hard. What else is written there?"

"Can you highlight that for Daniel?" Robert asked.

A few clicks of the mouse and there it was, right next to my own name: the maiden name of my wife, first, middle, and last, perfect Hebrew spelling, ten letters long.[3] The room fell silent. It was an extraordinary moment.

I fished a tattered index card out of my briefcase. "The Vilna Gaon, the famous eighteenth-century Lithuanian rabbi and scholar, made this seemingly bizarre statement about the Torah." I read from the card:

And the rule is that whatever was, is and will be to eternity is all included in the Torah from "In the beginning" to "in the sight of all Israel." And not just the generalizations, but even the particulars of each and every species, and each specific person, and everything that will happen to him from the day he is born to his end, and all his detailed particulars. And similarly every species of animal and beast, and every living creature in the world and every herb and plant and mineral and all the detailed particulars of every species, and of the particulars of the species to eternity, and what will happen to them and their roots.[4]

"He was saying that the Torah is not merely a text but also some sort of device into which vast amounts of information are compacted. At the time this must have sounded like some sort of magical fantasy or maybe just overzealous pride in the ancestral sacred book of the Jewish people. But these names embedded in the text of

Genesis 30 suggest to me that the Vilna Gaon was neither exaggerating nor fantasizing when he said the Torah was not written but created from a vantage point completely outside our dimension of time."

Robert had barely taken his eyes off the computer screen. "Is it only encrypted this way in the Leningrad Codex?"

"No. Thanks to the Masoretes, the Hebrew letter sequence shown above is exactly the same in every Torah scroll, in every Torah ark, in every synagogue in the world: the same one hundred forty-four letters in the same exact order. And this is just the beginning."

"What do you mean?" Dan asked.

"*Timotheus* is just the key code. Once I found it—and recovered from the shock—that key began to unlock other doors. That's why I refer to it as the chamberlain key. The chamberlain was the official in a royal household who held the key, on behalf of the king, that gave access to the most secret, guarded areas of the castle or palace. He opened doors no one else in the realm could. There's every reason to believe that what I've found is just the beginning. And it's not just personal information, although I'd like to begin by telling you something I discovered about the ancient name *Timotheus* that begins to explain what this is all about."

"Please do," Dan replied.

I took a deep breath and just came out with it.

"Okay. The Hebrew spelling of the ancient Greek name *Timotheus* is a marvel of meaningful synchronicity in and of itself. And there is no coincidence in the fact that it is indeed the only biblical name encrypted by equidistance in tight compaction in the Leningrad Codex. Its appearance in the book of Genesis is a singular phenomenon. No other single word or name of such length—nine letters or more—appears encrypted in such a way that it can be deciphered without the aid of some mechanical decryption device.

"Of course there was a very clear a priori condition for me to look for that exact name in that exact section of Genesis. Not much wiggle room here. I only have the one name. I was named after Timotheus, Paul's disciple as recorded in the New Testament. Hence my name: Timothy Paul. I am the father of six sons and a daughter, just like my father who has six sons and a daughter and just like Jacob who had six sons and a daughter with his wife Leah. Does this make me special or important? Absolutely not, but it is the sort of synchronicity that was bound to be noticed by me, particularly after the birth of my daughter.

"This internal equidistant structure was designed into the book of Genesis intentionally. And a sound empirical argument could be made that I was intended to recognize it sometime after the birth of my daughter when *all* of this biographical data finally synchronized. But I needed to know why. What did the name *Timotheus* really mean? It could not have been meant just for me. So what was the larger message?

"One day I came across an article in an academic journal that referred to various internal literary and poetic structures found in Latin, Greek, Arabic, and Hebrew texts. One of these structures was called *inverted parallelism*. It was a type of mirror writing in which the first line in a section of text was combined with, answered, or complemented by the last line. The second line was similarly related to the second-from-last line, the third to the third from last, and so on. By using this technique, one could discover the true meaning of the text.

"Another term for such constructions is *chiasm,* or *chiastic structure.* The same technique can be employed by mirroring words, hieroglyphs, or letters. As I learned more about this ancient device, I wondered if the *Timotheus* encryption exhibited a similar mirror-like structure. Rabbinic tradition clearly affirms that each letter of the Hebrew alphabet is also a word or hieroglyph in itself."

Robert piped in. "I read a very interesting book about this by Stan Tenen, about the Hebrew alphabet changing the world."

"Yes. I actually had a long phone conversation with Mr. Tenen, who has devoted his life to research on the ancient Hebrew alphabet. Anyway, since each of the Hebrew letters that made up the name *Timotheus* had a well-established symbolic meaning, it was easy to put my speculation to the test. Now take a look at this."

I took another page from my briefcase and laid it on the table. It showed that the Hebrew spelling of *Timotheus* was a perfect inverted parallel.

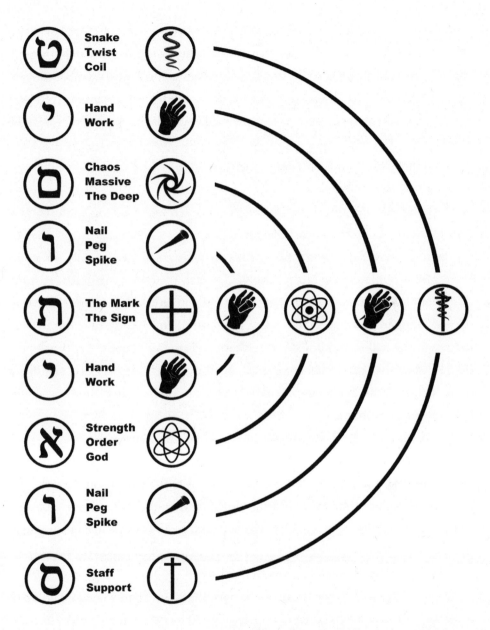

Figure 6.D. A chiastic representation of the Hebrew letters comprising *Timotheus* with their symbolic meanings.

"As you can see, the first letter in *Timotheus*—*teth*—represents a coil or snake, and the last letter—*samekh*—signifies a staff or support. As a first step toward a chiastic structure of this key, this was striking. Combining the two symbolic meanings together immediately evokes Jesus's words about Himself in John 3: 'As Moses lifted up the bronze snake on a pole in the wilderness, so the Son of Man must be lifted up.'"

Dan shook his head. "That's amazing."

"I agree," Robert exclaimed.

"It is indeed. And as you can see, the second letter, *yod* (meaning 'in the hand'), corresponds to the second-to-last letter in the word, *vav,* which represents a nail or peg, another image suggesting the One whose hands were pierced by nails. The third letter, *mem,* signifies chaos or the deep void, which matches up perfectly with the third-from-last letter, *alef,* which represents God and order. Here we get the notion of order being imposed upon the chaos. The fourth letter and the fourth-from-the-last repeat the nail-in-hand motif, so we have nails in both hands. And finally the central letter, *tav,* the symbol around which all the others are balanced, signifies a mark, sign, or cross. Perfect symmetry employed to combine simple root meanings to form a single cosmic message."

I paused. Both men had thoughtful looks but didn't comment.

"It looks to me like this is a mnemonic device par excellence, a compact mechanism to prompt our memory. The Son of Man has been lifted up on the cross and crucified as the means by which order is ultimately brought to an otherwise chaotic universe. This is a sign that represents the hope and promise made to all mankind at the very foundation of the world."

"Just amazing," Dan said for the second time.

"This was placed in the thirtieth chapter of Genesis, right where the house of Israel was first established, to signify the family and bloodline from which the Messiah would spring. I can only suppose that it is being exposed today to bear witness to all of humankind at this remarkable point in human history when information can be disseminated worldwide in an instant. It looks as if the brazen staff is once again being lifted up in the wilderness."

Robert was silent for a few moments longer as he stared carefully at everything I'd laid out on the table. Dan Murphy just shook his head in disbelief, seeming to wait for his friend's assessment.

At last Robert spoke: "Well, it darn sure looks like you've got *contact* here, Mr. Smith. And it seems pretty obvious who is sending the signals."

7

Who Are You?

Virginia, 2013

I wondered, after I had shared so many details from my puzzling journey and bizarre discovery, if I would ever see Dan and Bob again. So I was pleasantly relieved when Dan Murphy showed up in my gallery the following Saturday. I became a bit apprehensive, though, when he showed no sign of his typical good cheer. He seemed anxious, shaken even.

After a hurried handshake, Dan went right to the point: "Bob Dallet and I have taken a close look at the things you showed us last week, and we've been doing a bit of research of our own."

"Oh?"

"We've made some phone calls—nothing that would violate our agreement, of course—just getting the take of a few friends of mine on some of the general concepts you were sharing with us."

I felt the tension gathering in my stomach but didn't say anything.

"And, well, I have a funny question to ask. I hope you're not offended. It's just that we think this is very serious stuff, and there's something Bob and I would like to be sure about."

"Go ahead, Dan. I doubt that you will offend me." I sounded brave but was not so confident on the inside. "I know it all seems incredible, and I guess I'd be surprised if you guys didn't have some tough questions for me. But if customers walk in, I'm going to have to attend to them, just like I did last week."

"Why, certainly." He hesitated for a few moments before straightening himself, as if plucking up his courage. "Timothy, are you really who you say you are?"

At first I didn't answer. This was not a question I was expecting.

"I mean," he continued, "is Timothy Paul Smith your real name? And is that name on the sheet you gave us really your wife's name? And all the biographical information—your children, your family, the names, the dates, everything—is it all true?" He paused, waiting for me to speak. "Bob and I have to ask this because it all seems so impossible!"

"Dan, why would I make all that up? And *how* would I do it, even if I wanted to? I couldn't fabricate all those birth certificates!"

"No, I'm not saying that. It's just that it's all so hard to believe. Like I said, I made some phone calls and spoke to a friend, a research scientist in the pharmaceutical industry. I didn't give him any names or even mention the Hebrew Bible. I just gave him some comparable hypotheticals and said I'd found certain things in Webster's Dictionary about George Washington and his family, much like the things you found about your family in the Hebrew text."

I smiled and thought, *Dan is still a good investigative reporter.*

"I asked my friend if it could just be a bizarre coincidence. He said it was statistically impossible. That if such encryptions had been found in my edition of Webster's Dictionary, then Webster, or the company's printer, must have put them there intentionally."

I relaxed. Dan hadn't come to accuse me of fraud or to have me committed. "I know, Dan. Believe me, I know. When I first discovered *Timotheus* in the text— what I call the key code—years ago, before I really knew what it was, I did the same thing. I called a friend who was a professor of physical chemistry and gave him a hypothetical, except I said I'd found the encryptions in a newspaper. He told me the same thing your friend did."

"So." Dan swallowed. "It has to be God, then. Right?

I nodded in agreement.

"He's the only One who could do that," Dan said almost wistfully. "These days when a miracle happens, everybody thinks the person telling you about it is crazy. And, Timothy, that's what they're going to say about you if you go public. People will say you're nuts or that extraterrestrials must have contacted Moses or the Hebrew scribes. Or else they'll just say you fabricated all that biographical information."

"I don't think anyone will be able to say that I fabricated all those birth certificates. And I've never had any issues with my mental health. So I guess they'll have to fall back on outer space for an explanation."

We both laughed, some of the tension easing.

"And, like I told you the other day, I think what I've shown you so far is just the key code or passkey. That's just the beginning. I think I've only see the tip of the iceberg."

Now it was my turn to pause. I was thankful no customer had come through the door. I wanted to share more with Dan; he now seemed more of an ally.

"I'm in an awkward spot, Dan. If the encryptions in the Hebrew text had been about George Washington or Queen Isabella instead of me and my family, it sure would make things a lot easier. I could talk about them openly and publish whatever I wanted without people thinking I'm crazy or narcissistic or both. My family and I are living a nice quiet life in a peaceful little corner of the world. I've got an interesting career that pays the bills. I'm not looking for controversy, so I've been reluctant to talk about these things. Unless someone presses me, that is, like you've been doing."

"I hear what you're saying. But how could you keep this information under wraps forever? People should know about it!"

I shrugged. "I'm not so sure. And besides, would you want people thinking *you're* nuts? Or a megalomaniac?"

"But I thought you said you'd be open to talking to my astrophysicist friend."

"I am. But I'm also cautious, because some of the things I'm finding are pretty disturbing."

"What do you mean, 'disturbing'?"

Just then my two youngest sons walked in the front door of the gallery, toting their winter wetsuit duffle bags. "Surf's up, Dad," they said. They were meeting their sister here for a fine day of winter surfing.

I introduced them to Dan. "They've come in to make me feel bad about missing a great surf day," I said, then asked the boys to cover the shop for twenty minutes or so while Dan and I took a walk. "Okay, but no more than twenty minutes!" they stipulated.

As the two of us headed toward the harbor, I said, "Dan, listen. I've got twenty minutes to explain some things to you in private, so please don't interrupt me until I'm finished."

"I'm all ears."

"There have been odd things going on with the Masoretic text of the Hebrew Bible for at least a thousand years, but let's limit ourselves to modern times. Remember, Dan, the oldest known source of all of these observations that I've pointed out is the Leningrad Codex, written in about AD 1010. That codex is sitting in the National Library of Russia in Saint Petersburg. Since it's a book, not a scroll, it has an illuminated signature page cover, and I think that whoever created that beautifully decorated page knew about the key code, because its basic mathematical formulas were incorporated into the geometric design on the signature page with the names of all the scribes who worked on the transcription.[1] They must have known its importance, and I'm guessing that knowledge was passed down by the Masoretes, the same scribes who were so fanatical about maintaining the perfect letter sequence of the Hebrew Scriptures."

"Are you saying they knew about the name *Timotheus*?"

"I think so, and I also think they knew it was the key to unraveling other information in the text. That's why the rabbi and scholar Vilna Gaon said what he did, as if it were common knowledge among Torah scholars that the text was a storehouse of encrypted information. But until 1958 the Leningrad Codex was not the authoritative text; there was an older complete copy of the Masoretic text that had been protected—virtually unseen—in Aleppo, Syria, for hundreds of years by a Jewish community there. During the upheavals of World War II it was thought to have been lost or destroyed, but that may have been a ruse by Aleppo's Jewish community to keep black marketers from trying to get hold of it. Every square inch of it is worth a fortune."

"What happened to it?" Dan asked.

"In 1958 it was smuggled out of Syria and brought to Jerusalem, where it was secretly confiscated by the Israeli government. The president of Israel at the time was Yitzhak Ben-Zvi, a gifted Jewish historian, and the Aleppo Codex eventually ended up in the possession of the Ben-Zvi Institute. But by that time nearly the entire Torah section—much of Genesis through Deuteronomy—had been torn out."

"What? Why? How could such a thing happen? Why would anyone violate a sacred treasure of the Jewish people?"

I glanced around as if checking the area for eavesdroppers. "If I answered that, I'd have to throw you in the harbor. How do *I* know you're who you say *you* are?"

He blinked. When I saw my attempt at humor had failed, I smiled. "I'm kidding, Dan."

He smiled back. "Good. I don't swim so well. But seriously, why would anyone desecrate the oldest known copy of the Torah?"

"I can't be certain, but I have an idea. Not only was Ben-Zvi a historian, but his brother-in-law, Benjamin Mazar, was a famous archaeologist who specialized in artifacts related to the Bible. He conducted more digs in and around the Temple Mount in Jerusalem than anyone. Both men were intimately familiar with the claims of Jewish mystics and Torah scholars like the Vilna Gaon, who said emphatically that the Torah of Moses was encrypted with extensive information. They had no access to the Leningrad Codex, which was held under tight security at the time in the Soviet Union, but I think they wanted to remove and scrutinize the text of the oldest known Torah privately, without anyone knowing they had it. They could always claim that the Torah portion of the codex was missing when the codex fell into their hands. If the first five books had been stolen by anyone for profit en route to Israel, then sooner or later fragments would've shown up on the black market. And that hasn't happened.

"Whoever ended up with it wasn't interested in its monetary value; they wanted to keep it out of public circulation. They wanted time to crack the lock. In any case, the Torah section of the Aleppo Codex disappeared and has never been seen since, whatever the reason."

I stopped talking then and scanned the harbor, nearly empty except for a few traditional Chesapeake deadrise boats tied to the dock. The sun warmed our backs, a hint that spring was on its way. I already felt misgivings about saying so much to Dan. After all, he *had* been a Washington reporter. But I couldn't deny that it felt good to share some of the burden of all this information. And I knew that sooner or later I would have to tell the story to someone, and maybe Dan, who seemed sincere and supportive, was as good as anyone. I started leading the way back to the gallery. "But the Jews weren't the only ones looking," I said. "There was a long succession of people who suspected that some mysterious potential lay dormant in Jewish writings stretching back to the time of Moses. Why, even Isaac Newton was utterly convinced of it and spent his later years attempting to decrypt it."

"I know the Nazis were convinced of it. I did a piece on that in the late fifties. Very weird stuff."

"Yes, and the Nazis came late in the game. Many kings, emperors, and scholars over the last few thousand years have had at least some inkling that the Jews possessed something special, something they were protecting, something secret."

"What kind of secret are you talking about?"

Time was short—the boys would be anxious to go to the beach—so I spoke as quickly as I could. "Okay. Let's suppose for a moment that a number of Torah scholars, Kabbalists, and scribes over the centuries knew that one key to an encrypted text was 'honored of God.' They knew what the Greek name *Timotheus* meant. They knew there was no other name of such length—nine letters—written in a confined equidistance in the Torah. I even think some of them had deciphered the crucifixion chiasmus. They knew its presence was intentional, and they believed its meaning pointed to its role as a portal to unlimited knowledge: only by 'honoring God' could one unlock the Torah's hidden meanings. It would be dangerous for all mankind, especially for the Jewish people."

I watched as a single seagull buzzed the street, searching for a morsel of food. Then I continued. "Imagine, for example, if the Nazis had gotten hold of it. Their goal was the extermination of an entire race of people, not just a religion, but an entire bloodline that had been dispersed throughout many nations and cultures over time. What if the Torah did secretly contain all of the biographical details essential for identifying these people in the modern world, no matter where they'd been scattered, as the Vilna Gaon said?"

Dan shook his head. "You're right. It would have been a disaster if those monsters gained access to that information."

"And what of the scientific knowledge the Vilna Gaon referred to? And the Vilna Gaon probably knew something else as well, something that may have kept him from going crazy trying to crack the code himself. He probably knew that the information was protected by a time lock. Nearly all sacred sites in the ancient world were equipped with something like this, some sort of feature that restricted access or understanding to a specific moment, like a solar or astronomical event. But just like the West African textiles that Stella is so interested in, these ancient ceremonial sites are not the whole story. They're only a hint of something, reflections of rumors."

"So what's the time lock in this case? When does it open, and what do you think it will reveal?"

We stopped on the sidewalk in front of the gallery. I opened the door for Dan and followed him inside, where my sixteen-year-old daughter stood in her wetsuit with her short board under her arm. She wore an expression that told me I was late and that she had better things to do than hang around waiting for her father to finish talking to someone about his silly obsession. Dan and I were no sooner in the front door than she headed out the back.

"The time lock was apparently my family's biographical data. And my daughter—the seventh child, the final little cog in the gears—just walked out the back door. Now as far as what *else* will be revealed, well, I've already told you that what I've shared with you thus far is just the tip of the iceberg. But I'm trying to proceed cautiously. I think there's more than one time lock, and obviously those can't be forced open out of sequence."

Dan shook his head. "This is all hard to believe."

"No kidding."

8

Crossing the Delaware

Virginia, 2013

After my conversations with Dan Murphy and Robert Dallet, Dan continued to insist that I meet with the dean emeritus of engineering at Princeton University, Dr. Robert Jahn. Dan had interviewed the respected NASA astrophysicist in the midnineties.

With the help of some well-placed contacts of my own, I learned that Dr. Jahn had been involved in decades of research on the precognitive potential of human consciousness, some of which was quite controversial. The issue, as I would discover, was that this eminent scientist had organized and conducted experiments that some considered off-limits to respectable scientists (in spite of the fact that since the 1950s many major world powers—especially the United States and the Soviet Union—had been doing similar research, albeit secretly).[1] Also, according to at least two reliable sources, Dr. Jahn was part of a select group of scientists advising the US Joint Chiefs of Staff about exotic technologies.[2]

Dan arranged for me to meet with Dr. Jahn and some of his associates, and I agreed. While I welcomed Dan's enthusiasm, it also concerned me. I was afraid he might have promised I could spin straw into gold or build a workable time machine.

I knew my research and discoveries were fundamentally sound, but still I was taking a risk. I could potentially gain the support and assistance of scientists and experts in a wide range of disciplines. On the other hand, if they detected some fatal flaw in my approach or results, they could flatly reject everything I had done. From the moment I'd discovered what I now believed to be the key code, I knew I was out of my league on a scientific and technical level. And at this point I could really use some sound advice.

Dan and I drove together to Princeton, New Jersey, on a weekday and checked into the historic Nassau Inn. The evening before the meeting, I sat in the taproom of the Nassau Inn, staring at Norman Rockwell's *Yankee Doodle* mural behind the bar. I figured the most likely outcome of tomorrow's meeting was that I would make a fool of myself, much like the dandy on the wall. Regardless of my accomplishments in my own profession, I assumed that Jahn and his fellow academics would view me as little more than a treasure hunter. However, I believed I had found hard evidence that the Torah was indeed what the Vilna Gaon said it was: the greatest feat of information engineering the world had ever known, one that not only had overcome the limits of space in a way modern computer engineers could only dream about but had straddled the chasm of time as well. Although I was no fonder of an intellectual smackdown than the next person, I figured if that was where all this was leading me, I might as well get it over with.

IN THE SPOTLIGHT

On a beautiful spring morning Dan and I walked to our meeting at Dr. Jahn's home, just a few minutes from the Princeton campus. As we entered his spacious living room, I couldn't keep myself from seeing the midcentury modern decor as something I would expect for a retired academic of his age. I also couldn't help but notice the numerous giraffe paintings, sculptures, and photos in the room, even an eight-foot stuffed toy giraffe in the corner with its head scraping the ceiling. Nor could I keep myself from interpreting what I could from associated objects: *giraffes as anomalies.*

The entire group sat on a huge semicircular sofa, and after asking me if I preferred to be called Tim or Timothy, Dr. Jahn introduced himself and his colleagues by their first names. "We're not impressed with each other's degrees and titles, so there's no reason you should be."

"Fair enough," I said. "And please don't be impressed by my conspicuous lack of a title." The laughter that followed put me a little more at ease. I knew that Dan had already forwarded Dr. Jahn my curriculum vitae and family background, so I launched right into what I had planned to say.

"When I was born, I was given something that has turned out to be immensely more important than I could have imagined. It was my name, Timothy Paul Smith. I was raised Catholic and named in honor of Saint Timothy, protégé of the apostle Paul. I was the fourth son of six in a family that later included a girl, my sister. When my daughter was born sixteen years ago, it dawned on me that like my own father, I now had six sons and a daughter. I didn't plan it that way, of course; it just happened."

I suddenly realized that none of this was going to make any sense unless I mentioned my strange experience in the mountains of British Columbia in September 1989. I knew that if anything was going to give these folks cause to question my mental stability, that would do it, but I decided not to hold back. I recounted the episode as cogently as I could. One member of the group, a Jungian psychologist, asked a series of questions, pressing me to elaborate on particular elements of what she referred to as a classic archetypal encounter. Though I was generally familiar with Carl Jung's theories regarding archetypes and the collective unconscious and could see some connections to my experience, I thought Jung's perspective was inadequate to explain the many tangible results of the event.

However, my narrative helped to provide the scholars in the room with a general context. "That," I explained, "led me to seek out the Leningrad Codex. Because of my experience in the Canadian Rockies, I was under the impression that something had been covertly embedded in the text of the Torah, something waiting for me to come along and bring it to light. So after my daughter was born, I got my hands on an exact facsimile of the codex. Having read the book of Genesis many times and remembering that Jacob had six sons and then a daughter with his first wife, Leah, I figured that would be as good a place as any to start looking."

I quoted from memory the verses in Genesis that had started me down this path years before. I mentioned briefly my experiences with ancient and aboriginal ceremonial devices and the techniques they displayed for compacting information and of course the research of many academics who had discovered perplexing anomalies in the Torah and in biblical Hebrew going as far back as the thirteenth century.

I described how I had repeatedly encountered artifacts and documents that were directly related to these issues without going out of my way to look for them. I showed photographs of the African American ladder-back chair and the matrix-based arrangements on its needlework coverings. I gave my interpretation of West African iconography and its remarkably complex system of data compaction, and I went on to offer other examples of similar techniques commonly used in the ancient world not only in ceremonial devices but also in the architectural features of buildings, monuments, and temples.[3] I suggested that the origin of this technique, as far as I could trace, dated back to the ancient Hebrews.[4]

After talking for about an hour, I found to my surprise that no one had walked out or even rolled their eyes. So with rising confidence I moved beyond explaining why I had good reasons to suspect something important was waiting for me to what it was I had uncovered. On the large coffee table in the middle of the room I laid out various graphics and computer printouts. Beginning with my first discoveries, I explained the significance of the key code and demonstrated how it not only communicated a wealth of thematically correlated information but also revealed fundamental principles of encryption that would apply throughout the rest of the text. I answered questions and listened intently as members of the group offered insights and suggested possible avenues of future investigation.

I was still holding a lot back because in those early days I wanted to tread carefully, but still, as I spoke, a weight began to lift from my shoulders. I was finally beginning to remove the bushel basket from a lamp I had kept hidden for more than a decade. And I was relieved that—so far, at least—my information had been given a respectful reception. In fact, shortly after our meeting, Dr. Jahn and his colleague Brenda Dunne sent me a letter proposing a collaboration, saying, "The early results that Smith has presented to us are sufficiently impressive that we believe they should satisfy any objective person,"[5] and mentioned the possibility of a joint research project. I was grateful for the prospect of working with other people who were able and willing to help me explore the seemingly endless possibilities my investigation had opened up.

ON THE ROAD AGAIN

Thousands of red brake lights shimmered off the wet pavement, mixing with the amber glow of caution signs and the glare of headlights moving slowly in the opposite direction on Interstate 95. The main artery of the East Coast was clogged somewhere between Trenton and Philadelphia, slowing our return trip to Virginia's Eastern Shore. Rain continued to fall steadily, cocooning Dan and me in the SUV.

"Why the name *Timotheus*?" Dan rubbed his face and asked the question as if he had dreamed the Princeton meeting. "You showed them a little of what was encoded in the text, but you never explained why it was there. Why did it all start with *Timotheus*?"

"I'm not exactly sure." This had always been an awkward subject for me. I sometimes wished that any other phrase or name had been used.

"That can't be true. That name was chosen for a reason. If you don't have some idea as to why, then who does?" He nodded at the standstill traffic extending in both directions. "We've got plenty of time, so just tell me what you think, even if it's wild speculation. You can start out by explaining what you and Bob Jahn were talking about at lunch, the time-lock mechanism."

"Well, that part is pretty easy. A time lock is just a security device—"

"Yeah, I know generally what it is. You filled me in on our little walk by the harbor. But today you and Bob were talking about Stonehenge and some Egyptian temple or something. There was so much noise at the table I couldn't hear what you two were saying."

Traffic started moving again but at a crawl. "We were talking about how many ancient ceremonial structures were designed to operate as precognitive time-lock mechanisms. The simplest ones were based on solar and lunar cycles. If you could accurately predict those cycles, you could create architectural features that would, for instance, channel light from the rising sun down a narrow conduit on a specific day in the future, allowing it to shine on some otherwise hidden or obscure message or symbol—or whatever you wanted to keep secret until that precise moment."

"Yes, those features are amazing," Dan said.

"So whoever designed the original text from which the Leningrad and Aleppo codices were copied was using detailed biographical information from the distant future as a time-lock mechanism so that hidden information in the text could only stand revealed after those specific biographical events had taken place."

Dan cocked his head to one side and peered at me narrowly. "Now just slow down here and explain this time-lock thing more thoroughly so a simple Irishman can understand it. I think a lot hangs on this, at least to my way of thinking."

"You're right. In a way it does. The time lock is crucial," I conceded. "And when you look closely it provides some remarkable insight into much more than simply the mechanical workings of an encrypted manuscript."

"What do you mean?"

"Well, the encoded information is encrypted using precise mathematical sequences like the equal spacing of letters. Even an inverted parallel is based on symmetrical precision. That's how it functions mechanically, much like the equally spaced cogs of finely crafted clockworks, with all those precisely set gears and shafts and cogs synchronized so that the second, minute, and hour hands move at a predetermined speed. Some mechanical clocks are more complex than others and are designed to perform different functions, like simple or elaborate chimes, scenic displays of the seasons, or cycles of the moon and planets. And then there's the hidden cuckoo bird that leaps out and cuts loose with that obnoxious racket."

"That's when the text starts to play a more complex melody," Dan observed.

"That's a darn good analogy for a simple Irishman."

"Well, what made me think of it was a music box my aunt gave me for Christmas when I was little, with carved shepherd boys tending their sheep. I figured out how to wind it up, but I couldn't get it to play anything. I spent all of Christmas Day trying to get it to work. I thought it was broken at first, but my aunt just smiled and assured me it wasn't. Finally, I set it down and just stared at it. Eventually I noticed that the smallest shepherd, who was pointing to something in the sky, held a staff in his other hand. When I pulled it up from his clenched hand, I heard a little click, and at last the song began to play."

"That's a pretty tricky release pin. What song did it play?"

"'Greensleeves.' Been my favorite ever since."

"Well, there you go. That was a time lock set to release whenever tenacious little Danny finally figured it out. But these analogies just serve to point us in the right general direction. The reality is more fluid because you're dealing with divine influence and human free will. God could arrange for certain information to be woven into the Hebrew Bible in ways that could be detected by any person who was paying close enough attention."

Dan rubbed his chin thoughtfully.

"But if God wanted that information to be time locked or sealed," I continued, "then it would need to be opened up with a key code synchronized with precise information *that would only exist in the future.* And biographical information is the most precise because it consists of fixed points in time that are often a matter of record. The mechanism was set when the Hebrew letters were placed in their precise order by the first incarnation of the text, but the hands of time had to finally swing around until everything lined up in the future."

"And there had to be a way for someone to recognize it. In this case it was someone's name," Dan interjected.

"Yes. It appears the name was the trigger, all right."

"This must be a really important message if it needed all these locks and triggers," Dan said.

"I believe it is. But just as important is the way that it's being delivered. As I see it, anyway, the use of a time lock itself seems to confirm the existence of God."

"Yes, that's truly amazing. This seems to prove that the Hebrew Old Testament was not just divinely inspired but literally created by God."

Dan and I both sat quietly for a few long moments. As the traffic ahead of us began to move more easily, I broke the silence.

"Right. And once we accept that conclusion, we have to come to grips with the implications, including the notion that there could be much more specific and timely guidance in the ancient text than anyone previously assumed."

"I still can't get over the part about your wife's name," Dan said, shaking his head. "That would have done it for me."

"I was just thinking about that moment."

"I want to hear exactly how it happened, every detail."

"Is this how you got Jimmy Hoffa to tell his secrets, waiting until you had him stuck in traffic on I-95?"

"Absolutely. Standard procedure for investigative journalists."

"So when we were living on Martha's Vineyard in the late nineties, after I got hold of that facsimile copy of the Leningrad Codex, I knew what I was looking for and where I thought I'd find it. I ordered the encryption software and was so excited and antsy while I waited for delivery. So many memories and experiences and things I had learned and studied, especially about biblical Scripture, were being reshuffled and re-sorted in my mind. Things I thought I had forgotten. Things I had never understood that were starting to make sense."

I closed my eyes and summoned up details from years ago.

"When I got the software program installed, it was easy to locate the *Timotheus* key code. The software included an extensive lexicon with correct Hebrew spellings of all the biblical names in the Old and New Testaments, and it used the exact same spelling for *Timotheus* that I had. I tasked the program to search the entire Torah for the nine-letter name at every possible equidistant letter skip from one to a hundred thousand. The statistical-probability function in the software put the odds at well over a million-to-one for any random occurrence of that specific letter sequence. In just a few minutes the program located the *Timotheus* encryption in the text precisely where I had discovered it a month before in Genesis in the Leningrad Codex. And even though I expected it to be there, the moment was incredibly thrilling. But I was still really curious about something else."

"I'd be curious about a heck of a lot of stuff!" Dan laughed.

"I wanted to know exactly what the odds were of the nine-letter name being encrypted at such a minimal skip exactly where I was looking for it. It's that a priori thing. I wanted to be sure to avoid, you know, seeing what you want to see. So I tasked the program to search for the name only in that section that specifically mentioned Jacob's six sons and one daughter by Leah. The odds were mind boggling, many trillions to one. The computer was confirming what I already knew in my heart."

"I can't imagine what that was like."

"It's hard to explain what it feels like to encounter something like that. My mind was frantically searching for an answer that would account for the impossible."

Dan sat quietly for a few moments. "Where were you, exactly? Were you by yourself?"

"It was late at night. I had the computer set up in our bedroom and my wife was already asleep. There were no lights in the room except the glow of the monitor. I remember glancing over at my wife curled up in bed, sleeping peacefully. I had this crazy notion that if this was really something I was supposed to unravel and it was sealed with some sort of a time lock based on biographical data, then maybe, just maybe, her name would be there too. But that seemed beyond impossible. As you know, my wife has a long and unusual name. In fact, the correct Hebrew spelling of her first, middle, and maiden name would take too many Hebrew letters to fit inside such a tiny two-dimensional array—unless it were tightly compacted directly next to my own name."

"Tell me everything you remember."

"So I typed in her full name and clicked the mouse one time, Dan. *One time.* That's all it took for the bright red letters that spelled her name to appear in the vertical column next to my name, beginning in the exact same horizontal position. It was the most amazing thing."

"What did you feel at that moment?"

Dan had spent hours with me as I presented as logical an explanation as I could for something that was nearly impossible to explain, so I knew he wasn't asking for more of that. He was looking for me to speak from the heart, something that ran against instincts formed by years of professional habit. However, knowing how important Dan's faith was to him, I did the best I could, little though it was. "I was stunned. *Awestruck* might be a better word. Fearful too, but in an excited sort of way, like the moment when you first strap into a roller coaster at the state fair. And even though I had no idea where all this was leading, I knew I was going to hang on for the whole ride."

9

What's Going On?

Virginia, 2013

Several hours later than we expected, Dan and I arrived back at my gallery on the Eastern Shore. Drained and bleary eyed, we parted ways in hopes of salvaging some sleep from what was left of that night. After Dan shot me a text message to let me know he'd arrived home safely, I crawled into bed and slept like a rock until 10:00 a.m. After a shower and some coffee, I called one of my sons to cover the shop, then took a few hours to organize my notes and record my reflections on the meetings and activities of the last few days.

Honestly, as encouraging as the visit to Princeton had been, I was struggling with the reality that my very private quest for understanding was increasingly going public. Evidence that the Hebrew Old Testament included a divine revelation designed to unfold at a precise moment in history wasn't limited to the statistically impossible placement of a man's name and that of his wife. Other features established a sort of proof-positive condition in order to leave no question in the mind of a relatively receptive person. Among them was the fact that *Timotheus* was not only encoded in the Masoretic text against astronomical odds, but it was the only well-established ancient and biblical name embedded in the text that could be statistically demonstrated to have been encrypted intentionally.

The difficulty was that I had been mulling and researching these ideas for years while everyone else had to be brought up to speed all at once. And, of course, I was still being cautious about sharing the more sensational revelations that were emerging from the text. Still, I was glad to be enlisting the support of people comfortable enough in their own skins and with their own hearts to be able to go ahead, with me or without me, wherever things were leading.

And I still was not anywhere near feeling confident about where all of these events were headed.

I seemed caught up in a larger story but did not have any solid clues as to why my name and a significant amount of detail about me and other family members were in the Bible, of all places.

I was personally conflicted to the point that my wife urged me to see a therapist. Hopefully professional insight would relieve some of my questions and anxieties. So that's how I found myself sitting in a comfortable chair in a second-story office with pleasant posters on the walls, reassuring books on the shelves, and tropical fish serenely gliding around a tank. The therapist, a woman I judged to be about my age, smiled pleasantly as we navigated the paperwork, and she was still smiling as she asked her opening question.

"Do you prefer to be called Tim or Timothy?"

"Either one. Anything but Timmy. Only my mother calls me that."

"All right. I'll remember not to call you Timmy." Her manner was as serene as the fish in the tank. "I gathered from our phone conversation that things at home are a little bumpy for you right now. We can talk about that if you want, but first I'd like to ask if you have any questions for me before we get started."

"Actually, yes. I need to make sure that anything we talk about is absolutely private. I agreed to meet with you, but it wasn't my idea. This is something my wife wanted me to do, and I intend to make the most of it. But I want to understand how the confidentiality part works."

She nodded. "It can get a little complicated in some situations, but generally I can't share what I learn from our conversations with a third party unless I'm required to do so by law."

"That's about what I expected. Good enough."

"Anything else?"

"Yes. Something quite critical."

She encouraged me to continue, a serious expression on her face.

"Is it okay to call you Barbie or do you prefer Barb or Barbara?"

She laughed, and I leaned back in my chair. Actually, I was immensely relieved to have the chance to completely open up to someone, someone who was not emotionally invested in my life.

Over several sessions that followed, I started at the beginning and told her my story: the good, the bad, and the ugly. The ecstasy and the agony. My doubts and my fears. I spoke of the people I loved most and how painful and heartbreaking it was when they misunderstood or misjudged me. I told her of my dreams and visions and where they had led me.

I did hold off for a while, though, in telling her all about the chamberlain key.

A Stunning Finding

I was still learning new things nearly every day, proceeding carefully and methodically with my research, breaking things down to their most basic elements, and probing my conclusions cautiously. One of my discoveries, in particular, added yet another confounding bit of biographical information to my growing collection.

For me this stunning anomaly was perhaps as alarming as any observation I would find in the Hebrew Bible, and a great deal of time and effort was spent verifying its singular nature. I subjected it to every test of veracity I could think of but could not poke any holes in my methodology. Even now I am gripped by how inexplicable this is.

With my computer programs I did an analysis that revealed there was *only one* precise date—day, month, and year—that can be shown to be encrypted in the Hebrew text since the Gregorian calendar was reconciled with the Hebrew calendar in 1752. Figure 9.A reveals how this information appears in the Hebrew text.

נ ה ו ת י מ נ ה ו ה מ ז
ר א ת א ש ר ע ש ה ה י ה
ח ל כ ס מ כ ל א י ב י
ש ת ה ו י ש ב ת ה ה ב ה
ץ ו ח פ ר ת ה ה ב ה ו ש
ה ת ר ד מ ט ה מ ט ה ה
ס ב ת ו ע ב ת י כ ע י
ה נ י ם נ ש א י ה א ר
י ר ו י נ ג ע ו י ה ו
ע נ ב ו מ כ ל ה ה ר י ה
ת י ה ו י ב ל ע ס ו ב
י ש ל ח ס ו י ל כ ו א
ע נ י ה י ו ש ב ב ג ז

Figure 9.A. Vertically, bottom to top: *23/Sh'vat/5720*
("on the twenty-first day of February 1960").

That date is February 21, 1960, the day I was born.

Once again I asked myself, *Just what is going on?*

Throughout the course of my career, I'd explored and investigated many unusual historical artifacts that had led me off the beaten path, but those adventures could be easily shared and appreciated by others. But for this one I simply struggled to find the words. The stunning statistical realities were impressive. They would probably be convincing to seasoned mathematicians and engineers, but how was I to explain to my wife and children, several of them still teenagers at the time, that not only was my life intertwined with some ancient manuscript but their lives were too?

The emotional and personal tide was rising around me faster than I could adjust to, and in my own ruminating on all these things, I wondered if there were only two possibilities: either I was going crazy or I was already gone.

Here I was, again sitting in Barbara's office in that comfortable chair. We were now deep in discussion of the chamberlain key and what I had discovered in the Hebrew text. Barbara seemed very interested, and I couldn't tell if she was just being professionally polite or if she actually wanted to understand. But when I told her about my meetings with scientists, scholars, agents, and publishers and she saw the pace of my life accelerating, her questions became even more probing. She seemed to have things she longed to know, unanswered questions of her own.

"Tim, all these things in the text—the codex, whatever—the things that sound so Christian. You said the document was written in the Middle Ages, only a thousand years ago. Couldn't those things have been slipped into the text by—"

"A crafty monk or a scribe or even the Catholic or Orthodox Church? Like someone using some kind of multigeared hand-powered encryption machine?" I was being a bit snarky, but thankfully that didn't faze her.

"Right. I mean, a lot of it sounds like that sort of thing could have happened."

"It's possible that some of these things were inserted in the Christian era. But there would still be serious problems with that theory. For instance, whoever did this seems to have had detailed knowledge of the future or was able to affect certain events in the future."

"Right, the biographical stuff. I keep forgetting about that. That's how you got on to this to begin with. And I want to ask you about that because I'm concerned about how you handle that emotionally."

So that's what we did. We talked for some time that day and in future sessions about how it felt to be attempting to share what I knew was a major, inexplicable discovery that just happened to have me right in the middle of it. Was I some kind of narcissist looking for a way to find my moment of fame?

No way, José. But just what was going on?

ANOTHER AVENUE OF TRUTH

Above all, I believed that everything I had encountered thoroughly confirmed that the text of the Hebrew Scriptures could be relied upon as accurate in their scribal transmission, validating their immense value as divine guidance and instruction. It excited me to have such clear evidence of the divine source of the Hebrew text. It intrigued me to anticipate that perhaps many key passages in the New Testament could be interlinked with the coded structures of the Old Testament like two halves of a locket, providing yet another layer of understanding. In fact, the entire Judeo-Christian canon was looking more and more like a stack of transparencies wherein detail and definition could be applied by laying one transparent leaf upon another, never obscuring or altering the information on the preceding leaf.

I also couldn't help but wonder if, just as Jesus used parables to illustrate concepts some of His listeners might find difficult to grasp, the matrices that were layered and interwoven into the Hebrew text were yet another way for God to convey truth to human beings.

I felt certain it could not be of any small significance that the text used to do so was the source text for every Torah scroll in every ark in every synagogue throughout the world. But by nature and by training, I knew I had to regroup and reevaluate. I knew it was folly to assume I could perfectly comprehend anything God might be doing, but I needed to ask (and do my best to answer) a series of fundamental questions. And the first of these was, What did I know—or be-lieve—was going on?

There could be little doubt I was witnessing something of great importance, something miraculous even. The things I had discovered had begun with very per-sonal information about me and my family—the chamberlain key that got my at-tention, drew me in, and drove me to investigate further. But apart from that, it had become clear that this was not about me. I was just an entryway, a means of accessing a series of codes that could be objectively observed by almost anyone in the world, given the current state of information technology.

While some could possibly look at these things and pass them off as mere coin-cidences or curiosities, my personal and professional background, not to mention the otherwise inexplicable added dimension of my dreams and their correspondence to various points in the story, made it impossible for me to dismiss what I had observed. That didn't mean I understood it fully. It did mean, however, that I had to acknowl-edge that something unique and important was happening and that I was a part of it somehow.

Besides, I was already aware of something more about the key code that I had not yet discussed with anyone, something likely to get me into trouble with a great many people.

Although the initial code markers I discovered in the Hebrew text of the Lenin-grad Codex related specifically to me and my family, I quickly learned that the mes-sages those things pointed to had no more to do with me than with anyone else in the world, past or present. My biographical data points, impossible to contrive or falsify,[1] were mere signposts. They allowed someone living in the modern age of computers to recognize that something incredible was interwoven into an ancient document, a document that for centuries had been repeatedly rumored to possess miraculous qualities.

As you might imagine, I struggled to understand why that someone should be

The store at Germansen Landing, British Columbia, more than two hundred miles
north of Prince George, Canada, near where I experienced the vision that changed my
life and eventually led to the discovery of the chamberlain key.

An illuminated "carpet" (decorative) page from the Leningrad Codex. The handwriting includes the names of the scribes who copied the Hebrew Scriptures that comprise the codex. The middle of the star is a blessing.

Artist's depiction of the Virgin of El Rocío appearing to the hunter in the stump of a tree in the thicket.

The statue of the Madonna of El Rocío, a statue carved from wood,
on display in the Hermitage of El Rocío near Almonte, Spain.

This page and the next: the sixteen icons, seen only on close observation, in the circular decorations that surround the Madonna of El Rocío statue on the previous page.

ט י ט ה ל ו א פ ת ע י ק ו
י ה ו ה צ ב א ו ת ש י מ ו
י ר נ י כ א ש י ש ר י ע
כ י ע ת ה ר א י ת י ב ע י
א י ס מ ע ל י ר ו ש ל מ ו ע
י ע נ י א ל ה י כ י ה כ י
י ד ג ו ר ל י ח ב ל י ם נ
ל ד ב ג י א צ ל מ ו ת ל א
ו י ה י ה ו א צ ו א ה ו י ע
ש כ י ג ר א נ כ י ע מ ד ת
י ו ן פ י י ד ב ר ח כ מ ו
ב ל ו ל ת מ ס י ה ל ד נ פ
נ ו א ל ל מ ו ש ע ו ת ו ל
מ א ו ר ו ש מ ש א ת ה ה צ
ה ע ד י ס ו א ל נ ה ר י ו

Vertically, bottom to top: *institution, Nazi,* and *a mirror.* The horizontal letters correspond to a date that translates to September 11.

Google Translate box depicting the translation of the vertical phrase.

Artist's depiction of the "Woman Clothed with the Sun"
and the great red dragon of Revelation 12.

me, since I knew better than anyone that I wasn't extraordinary. I wasn't especially bright or gifted. Any success I had achieved in life was largely due to persistence, happenstance, and family legacy. I had failed at enough things, public and private, to firmly establish that fact. On the other hand, I couldn't deny I possessed certain personality traits and experiences that perfectly prepared me for the strange discoveries I was making.

MOST HIGH GOD

One aspect of the key code that I had not revealed that day to the experts at Princeton—the thing that had finally let me know what all of this was really about—involved something that had irrevocably altered history once before and now appeared poised to shift the course of world events again. The discovery I was keeping close to my chest, so to speak, had to do not with me but with someone else, someone so unique that finding a single name to describe him was a difficult task. Someone who "honored God" and was also "honored of God," fitting the true meaning of the ancient Greek compound word *Timotheus*.

Intersecting the *Timotheus* key code horizontally—in perfect symmetry and forming a symbol easily recognized in the ancient and modern world—was another name, one that has been the subject of much speculation and debate. The name in Hebrew is *Elohim Alef Tav*. *Elohim* is the name first used for God in the Hebrew Scriptures; it is commonly translated into English as "God" but also carries the connotation of "True God" or "Most High God." *Alef* is the first letter in the Hebrew alphabet (we get our English word *alphabet* from the first two letters, *alef* or *aleph* and *bet*), and *tav* is the last letter in the Hebrew alphabet.

In other words, the phrase transecting *Timotheus* in Genesis where I found the key code reads "True God: Alpha and Omega" (see Figure 9.B). And we have already seen that *Timotheus* is an inverted parallel depicting the Crucifixion, quite obviously a reference in the Torah, the Old Testament—a book written centuries before His birth—to none other than Jesus Christ.

מ ר ל א ה ז ב ד נ י א
ת י ז ב ד ט ו ב ה פ ע
נ י א י ש י כ י י ל ד
ש ה ב נ י ם ו ת ק ר א
ז ב ל ו ן ו א ח ר י ל
ת ק ר א א ת ש מ ה ד י
כ ר א ל ה י ס א ת ר ח
ע א ל י ה א ל ה י ם ו
ת ר ח מ ה ו ת ה ר ו ת
ת א מ ר א ס ף א ל ה י
פ ת י ו ת ק ר א א ת ש
פ ל א מ ר י ס פ י ה ו
א ח ר ו י ה י כ א ש ר

Figure 9.B. Vertical: the key code (*Timotheus*). Horizontal: *Elohim,* right to left, followed by *Alef* and *Tav*. The two Hebrew letters directly following *Timotheus* in the matrix are *Kaf* and *Yod,* shown at the bottom. Together, they make the sound *ki* and translate into the word *key* in more than thirty-five languages.

10

An Unlikely Candidate

Virginia, 2014

After a number of sessions, I now felt very comfortable sharing openly with Barbara, my therapist. I felt I was making good progress in becoming more comfortable with the odd set of circumstances in my life—and what I might have to face when I started sharing the facts to a broader public. And she and I were having increasingly more complicated conversations about what I had found in Genesis and elsewhere in the Bible. Barbara was particularly interested in who might have been able to plant some coded information in the Hebrew text.

"So, Timothy, could someone, maybe a *crafty* monk, have been behind this?" she asked.

"Well, remember, the Masoretic text is the text that the Hebrew scholars themselves believe is the most accurate. Their traditions say that this is the perfect or near-perfect letter sequence, dating from well before the time of Jesus. It is the exact same Torah text that is cherished and protected in every Torah ark in every synagogue in the world. If it was manipulated or encoded in the Middle Ages, then the Jews did it. The care and keeping of the text have always been in their hands."

"Okay, but if this had been done by a Jewish scribe or rabbi, why would it refer to Jesus and Mary and so on?"

"Well, Jesus was Jewish. The first Christians were Jews. And the theme of a coming Messiah loomed large in the Jewish Scriptures. I think I understand what you're saying, though. It would have been odd for a medieval Jewish scribe to insert references to Jesus and Mary. But even if that had been the case, this could not have been achieved by any known human technology, either then or now."

She seemed genuinely perplexed. I knew nothing about Barbara's religious background or beliefs or anything about her personal life. I supposed that was the therapist protocol. But I wondered what aspect of my research and discoveries she was struggling with.

"Barbara, what do you really want to know? As I've said, this has run through a number of pretty critical gauntlets, and soon it will all be laid on the table for anyone and everyone to comment on it, critique it, or laugh at it. But this is no magic trick, like trying to predict the next nuclear disaster or stock-market crash. This is deeper than all that. And the more I look at it, the deeper it seems to get. I can no longer keep it to myself. This is something I have to do."

"I understand. But have you really thought through the consequences of making all this public? I mean, there are a lot of disturbed people out there. Trust me on that. And just from what I know about it, I think you're going to be in for quite a ride."

She was right. That was the crux of the matter.

Unlikely Characters

As I hope I have already made clear, I am not a linguist. I'm not a Hebrew scholar. I'm not a theologian. I'm not a mathematician or computer scientist. I have a fairly narrow and arcane area of expertise. So in addition to asking questions like "What's going on?" and "Is it possible?" I have had to wrestle repeatedly with the question "Why me?"

With renowned scholars and scientists like Eliyahu Rips investigating the Hebrew text, why would I have the temerity to think that I have a role to play in this fascinating and ongoing field of study? There are others, too numerous to mention, who would have made far better candidates, people of great learning, spiritual sensitivity, and professional prominence.

Of course, even as I pose these questions, I remember that the Bible is replete with accounts of people asking much the same thing. When God commissioned Moses to lead the Hebrews out of slavery in Egypt, Moses responded, "Who am I to appear before Pharaoh? Who am I to lead the people of Israel out of Egypt?"[1] When the angel of the Lord appeared to Gideon and told him to rescue God's people from the oppression of the Midianites, Gideon answered, "How can I rescue Israel? My clan is the weakest in the whole tribe of Manasseh, and I am the least in my entire family!"[2] When God called Jeremiah to be His prophet in Jerusalem, Jeremiah said, "I can't speak for you! I'm too young!"[3]

Over and over the Bible depicts unlikely, unworthy, undistinguished candidates who have been thrust into surprising roles. Saul was hiding among the equipment when it was time for Samuel to anoint him as the first king of Israel. David was carrying cheese to his warrior brothers just before facing Goliath. Esther was being groomed for the king's harem before she became the queen. So perhaps my part in the drama of the chamberlain key is simply explained: God specializes in using unlikely characters.

Daniel is another example in the Bible of an unlikely character rising to play an unexpected role. His story is also an account that reveals a mysterious message nestled inside another mysterious message. The fifth chapter of the book of Daniel tells of a lavish feast Babylon's King Belshazzar[4] hosted for himself and his nobles, a crowd of a thousand. As the festivities progressed and the wine flowed freely, he ordered that the gold and silver chalices his predecessor Nebuchadnezzar had plundered from the temple of Yahweh in Jerusalem nearly seventy years earlier be brought to the feast. When the holy relics arrived, he and his nobles, his wives, and his concubines drank wine from them while praising the gods of Babylon.

Suddenly what looked like a human hand appeared in the room. It began etching letters on the wall of the king's palace illuminated by the flames of a nearby lampstand. The raucous partygoers fell silent. As the king watched the hand move through the air and make mysterious marks on the wall, he paled and then collapsed into his royal chair. After a few moments, the writing ceased and the hand disappeared.

The king shouted an order, his voice shaky: "Summon my enchanters, soothsayers, and astrologers! Bring them here! Now!"

Moments later the court magicians stumbled into the king's presence. Belshazzar pointed to the strange shapes on the wall. "Whoever reads this message and shows me what it means will be dressed in royal robes and be given a gold chain of authority to wear around his neck! I will make him the third most powerful man in this kingdom" (presumably after Belshazzar and his father, the co-regent, Nabonidus). As the assembled sages looked from the king to the wall and back again, their brows furrowed. They stepped closer to the image. They viewed it from various angles. They whispered together. Finally, they turned to the king and began to make excuses for their inability to make sense of the mysterious writing.

Belshazzar shouted for silence and rose from his chair, but before he could give voice to his frustration, the queen mother appeared in the room and bowed low. "Long live the king! . . . There is a man in your kingdom who has within him the spirit of the holy gods. During Nebuchadnezzar's reign, this man was found to have insight, understanding, and wisdom like that of the gods. Your predecessor . . . made him chief over all the magicians, enchanters, astrologers, and fortune-tellers of Babylon. This man Daniel, whom the king named Belteshazzar . . . can interpret dreams, explain riddles, and solve difficult problems. Call for Daniel, and he will tell you what the writing means."

In moments, it was done. Daniel was ushered into the king's presence. Belshazzar told him what had happened, how the king's magicians and mystics had failed, and then repeated his offer of wealth and power if Daniel could read and interpret the message. Daniel agreed to explain the message, but first he reminded Belshazzar how God had humbled his predecessor Nebuchadnezzar, whose power and wealth had made him arrogant.

Daniel said, "You knew all this, yet you have not humbled yourself. For you have proudly defied the Lord of heaven and have had these cups from his Temple brought before you. You and your nobles and your wives and concubines have been drinking wine from them while praising gods of silver, gold, bronze, iron, wood, and stone—gods that neither see nor hear nor know anything at all. But you have not honored the God who gives you the breath of life and controls your destiny! So God has sent this hand to write this message."

Daniel then turned to the writing on the wall, which consisted of four words: *Mene, mene, tekel,* and *parsin.* Daniel told the king that *mene* meant "numbered," because "God has numbered the days of your reign." *Tekel,* he said, translated as "weighed," meaning "you have been weighed on the balances and have not measured up." And the final word, *parsin,* meant "divided," signifying that Belshazzar's kingdom would be "divided and given to the Medes and Persians."

You can imagine the reception for this dire message. When Daniel finished speaking, silence filled the room. The court held its breath in anticipation of the king's fury, but to everyone's surprise, Belshazzar ordered that Daniel be dressed in royal robes and given a gold chain of authority and proclaimed him Babylon's third in command. That same night, however, King Belshazzar was killed, and Darius the Mede ascended to the throne, fulfilling the promise of the mysterious message on the wall.

The famous scene of Belshazzar's feast exhibits so many parallels to things I had observed in the text of the Hebrew Bible that they hardly need pointing out. But something else was hidden in the text of Daniel 5 that, when brought to light, helped me understand it a little better. Perfectly intersecting the beginning of verse 5—"Suddenly, they saw the fingers of a human hand writing on the plaster wall of the king's palace, near the lampstand. The king himself saw the hand as it wrote"—lies another encryption at an equidistance of ninety-seven. It reads "Timothy intelligence." This is the English spelling of Timothy rendered in six-letter Hebrew. The Hebrew word *leb* that follows "Timothy" could also be rendered as "mind," "will," "heart," "soul," or "conscience." It is a word often used in biblical Hebrew to mean "the very heart or essence of the matter."

A three-letter word intersects that phrase. It is the word *wrote.* The symbol formed by this intersection can be considered a hieroglyph, its meaning made plain by its placement in the verse:

Figure 10.A. Vertical, top to bottom: "Timothy intelligence." Horizontal, right to left: "wrote."

A fair interpretation of this hieroglyph could be "The mind/will/intelligence of He who is honored of God wrote . . ." We could play around with the syntax to make it more pleasing in English, but that seems unnecessary. We have already established that Timothy, when used as an equidistant code, is a reference to Elohim Alef Tav; that is, God. So the message hidden in the text referring to the mysterious message written on the wall could be understood as "The writing on the wall emanated from the mind and will of God."

A SPECIAL LANGUAGE FOR THE COMPUTER AGE?

As I have thought about the unique messages the key code has revealed in the Hebrew text, is it too much to infer from these remarkable "coincidences" that God may be seeking to communicate with us in a special language, one that is based on empirical things like logic, mathematics, and statistics but in its own way is simultaneously strange, wonderful, and mystical?

Is it possible that just as Daniel read and understood the writing on the wall as if it were a first-grade reader, we might be able to grasp, with the assistance of modern technology, messages that have long been inaccessible to human understanding?

Could it be that God, who not only uses human language but also employs dreams, visions, metaphors, symbolism, parables, and more to communicate with people, might use numbers and computers and mathematical sequences too?

To the ancient Hebrews, God communicated in Hebrew. The New Testament writings spoke to the Hellenistic world of Jesus's day in Greek. Might God have foreseen and planned to speak to the age of computers in ways that could be fully parsed only with the use of computers?

If God *is* God, would He not be capable of such an endeavor?

In his fascinating book *Coincidences in the Bible and in Biblical Hebrew*, professor Haim Shore draws attention to a number of remarkable anomalies in the Hebrew Bible that he insists are very meaningful. His book describes case after case of statistically significant coincidences that, if taken in context, not only suggest a deeper meaning of the biblical narrative but also demonstrate advanced understanding of scientific principles. Dr. Shore explains that the meaningful coincidences in biblical Hebrew are not only a sign or signature of divine authorship but also a language of divine communication.[5]

In other words, could apparent coincidences in the Hebrew text be not random but meaningful? Might they constitute an old-but-new means of divine communication? Could statistically significant intersections of words and phrases in the carefully preserved Hebrew text of the Bible be a way of getting our attention, turning up the volume, and emphasizing things God wants us to know now, in *this* generation?

PART III

MYSTERIOUS MADONNA

The Matrix Turns

Virginia, 2014

Since my discovery of the chamberlain key, I have had to accept the reality that the Hebrew text will never stop amazing me. I believe it is perhaps a limitless storehouse of details, information, and wisdom—and surprises, which don't always fit in the tight religious boxes I and others are more comfortable with. So I should not have been caught too off-guard by what I found one morning while searching the text.

It was a Tuesday. It's easy to remember the day because a friend of mine, Dr. Arthur Fournier, always comes into my gallery on Tuesdays. He has a regular Tuesday breakfast meeting and almost always stops by afterward to shoot the breeze. In addition to a distinguished medical career, Arthur is the author of the book *The Zombie Curse,* which chronicles his twenty-five-year battle against the AIDS epidemic in Haiti and South Florida.[1]

Since his retirement on Virginia's Eastern Shore, Arthur had become fascinated with the West African influence in the Chesapeake region reflected in early decorative ironwork and textiles, particularly the form and function of African American ladder-back chairs (a subject he researched extensively and in which we shared a common interest). But it was no chair I wanted Dr. Fournier to look at on this particular day.

I waved him to my desk to look over my shoulder at the computer monitor. "What do you make of this?"

"That's the *Timotheus* encryption in the Torah. See? I'm picking up a bit of Hebrew."

"Yes, that's what it is, but take a look at this." I set a function on the program to search exclusively over and on top of the line of letters in the same vertical column as the key code and only inside the same small sixteen-line matrix. "I was reading this morning about DNA possessing codes on top of codes, and I was just wondering . . ."

"If you were wondering if anything was written directly on top of the *Timotheus* key code, it would have to be at an extremely low equidistance to fit in the matrix," Arthur said.

I nodded. "Yes, exactly. How about an equidistance of two?"

"That would be as low as it gets." He chuckled.

I set the search function to scan over the top of the key code at an EDLS of two and only for words in the database of five letters or more. It took only a split second for the powerful program to inspect that minute section of the matrix—and to identify *ten* perfectly spaced letters that made up not a word but a *name*. The program highlighted the ten Hebrew letters in red and gave the English translation in the sidebar. It was a name I had known virtually nothing about until just a few hours earlier.

"It can't be!" The name was clearly familiar to Dr. Fournier. "The *Rocío Madonna*!"

If I had been raised anywhere in the Spanish-speaking world, the phrase would have been a household name. Arthur, on the other hand, had a better working knowledge of medieval Spanish history than I. He began snapping his fingers and rattling off a dozen mind-bending connections between the famous Virgin of El Rocío legend and the Leningrad Codex. He nudged me out of my chair, commandeered my computer, and in no time brought up a transcript of the oldest written account of the legend,[2] which initiated nearly eight hundred years of veneration and pilgrimages to the Hermitage of El Rocío in the town of Almonte, Spain, attracting a million people every year to the Spanish province of Huelva. I listened as he read the tale aloud and watched him grow more excited as he got to the part about the hunter.

A man out hunting, finding himself at the end of the town of Almonte, was alerted by the sound of vehement barking dogs. By this he was directed to a place covered with brambles and thorns into which he struggled to discover the cause of alarm. To his amazement he discovered an intact image of the Blessed Virgin Mary clothed with a white linen tunic adorned with green, setting on the stump of a tree. She was wondrous and beautiful beyond even the most liberal imagination.

The hunter was beyond joy and took pains to remove the image and place her upon his shoulders and take her some three leagues distant to the town of Almonte, whereupon he collapsed with fatigue. When he awoke the sacred image was gone, causing him great sorrow. When he returned to the place where the image was discovered he beheld again the Virgin on the tree stump. He alerted the clergy and the town council, who all came to pay devotion and respect.

In the very spot where the image was discovered, the hunter built for himself a small hermitage not ten yards long and also built a shrine and placed the image on the tree stump and thereafter adoring her in that place in the name of Madonna of Rocinas.[3]

Arthur explained that one common cord tying the Leningrad Codex and the Rocío Madonna together was the famous Alfonso X of Castile, better known to history as Alfonso the Wise. This thirteenth-century Spanish king surrounded himself with Jewish scribes who translated the most important literary works of the medieval world, especially the Hebrew Scriptures, into his native Castilian language in order to fulfill his goal of making these classic works available to his subjects.

Arthur's voice vibrated with excitement. "The Hebrew scribes in Spain in the thirteenth century were steeped in Jewish mysticism. Alfonso X may have started it all. He was an ardent devotee of the Virgin Mary, and it wouldn't surprise me if he had a hand in the creation of the legend. How weird is it that *codex* in Latin means 'tree stump' and that you've found the Rocío Madonna in the codex?"

Figure 11.A. Artist's depiction of the Virgin of El Rocío appearing in the stump of a tree in the thicket.

I loved brainstorming with Arthur. It was true that my knowledge of the Rocío Madonna legend and the Castilian king's connection to it was newly acquired, but I had been exploring the possibilities for many hours just before my friend's visit.

I asked for my swivel chair back. "That's weird, Arthur, I'll grant you. But not as weird as this." I opened my software program again.

I explained to him that I had recently taken up the notion that if massive amounts of intelligent information were encrypted into small portions of the text, then at one point you would run out of mathematical possibilities within a matrix comprised of just a few hundred symbols. But this limitation would fade if the matrix were turned like a dial, using precise multiples and divisions. Every degree of rotation would reshuffle the fixed set of letters and produce additional possibilities. In this way information could be written on top of information.

In Hebrew (as in many other languages) the word *matrix* is synonymous with the word *cervix,* conveying the idea of something that expands and contracts around a fixed center. So I manipulated the program to expand the matrix to exactly double its size. Instead of sixteen vertical columns, I divided the same letters into thirty-two columns. The result was astounding.

I highlighted only the letters that lay in a perfectly symmetrical cross in the matrix, centered precisely on the same *qof* and *yod* in the codex, the letters that translate to "key" in numerous languages. *Rocío* now appeared in a single vertical line from top to bottom above the key, and *Madonna* appeared in a single vertical line from bottom to top, below the key.

Because I knew that Arthur (or anyone else, for that matter) would have a hard time simply taking my word for it, I opened Google Translate, an online service anyone can access. The perfectly balanced crossbar translated right to left as follows: "Her womb opened, and she conceived and brought forth a son."

Another translation program rendered it as "Her matrix opened, and she conceived and bore a son." Though I had known what the translation would reveal, it was nonetheless exciting. The atmosphere in the room was electric.

"So who was 'the son' that the Virgin of El Rocío brought forth?" I asked.

Arthur pointed. "I see it! I can read that much Hebrew. It's resting perfectly on the bar of the cross: *Elohim Alef Tav!*" *Elohim,* First and Last.

ללאהותההרותלדדליעקבבןחמ
נתןאלהימשכריאשרנתתישפ
ראשמוישׁשכרותהרעודלאהו
קבותאמרלאהזבדניאלהימא
סיזבלניאישיכיילדתילוש
אתשמוזבלונואחרילדההבתו
נהויזכראלהימאתרחלוישמ
יפתחאתרחמהותהרותלדבןו
סאתחרפתיותקראאתשמויוס
הליבןאחרויהיכאשרילדהר
מריעקבאללבןשלחניואלכה
ציתנהאתנשיואתילדיאשרע
אלכהכיאתהידעתאתעבדתיא
מראליולבןאםנאמצאתיחןב
יברכנייהוהבגללדויאמרן

Figure 11.B. *Rocío* appears vertically from the top down; *Madonna* appears vertically from the bottom up. Horizontally (right to left): "Her womb opened, and she conceived and brought forth a son."

ל ל א ה ו ת ה ה ר ו ת ל ד ד ל י ע ק ב ב ן ח מ
נ ת ן א ל ה י ם ש כ ר י א ש ר נ ת ת י ש פ
ר א ש מ ו י ש ש כ ר ו ת ה ה ר ע ו ד ל א ה ו
ק ב ו ת א מ ר ל א ה ז ב ד נ י א ל ה י ם א
ס י ז ב ל נ י א י ש י כ י י ל ד ת י ל ו ש
א ת ש מ ו ז ב ל ו ן ו א ח ר י ל ד ה ה ב ת ו
נ ה ו י ז כ ר א ל ה י ם א ת ר ח ל ו י ש מ
י פ ת ח א ת ר ח מ ה ו ת ה ר ו ת ל ד ב ן ו
ס א ת ח ר פ ת י ו ת ק ר א א ת ש מ ו י ו ס
ה ל י ב ן א ח ר ו י ה י כ א ש ר י ל ד ה ר
מ ר י ע ק ב א ל ל ב ן ש ל ח נ י ו א ל כ ה
צ י ת נ ה א ת נ ש י ו א ת י ל ד י א ש ר ע
א ל כ ה כ י א ת ה י ד ע ת א ת ע ב ד ת י א
מ ר א ל י ו ל ב ן א ס נ א מ צ א ת י ח ן ב
י ב ר כ נ י י ה ו ה ב ג ל ל ד ו י א מ ר נ

Figure 11.C. *Elohim Alef Tav* is highlighted above the crossbar that includes the phrase *Rocío Madonna*.

I wasn't finished. "Now look at this." I opened a picture file I had saved earlier that morning.

Arthur nodded. "That's her. I've never been to Almonte, but I've seen this before. That's the way the Rocío Madonna statue looks today. Maybe you should pay her a visit, Timothy."

"I may. I have some questions I'd like to ask the Loyal Brotherhood."

"Who?"

"It's reportedly a fraternity that venerates the legend and the statue. The elaborate chapel, in its many incarnations, and the adornment of the statue are all their doing. They've been watching over and protecting this exact spot in southern Spain since the Middle Ages."

"I bet Alfonso X was the charter grand master of the Loyal Brotherhood."

I shrugged. "Could be. And I'd love to know if it was Alfonso the Wise who insisted on this little touch." I reached for a pencil and carefully tapped the monitor, counting for Arthur the circular decorative elements framing the Madonna statue. I knew, of course, there's no such thing as random mathematics and geometry when it comes to secret fraternal orders, and the distinctive floral motifs were unlikely to be an exception. "Sixteen," I announced.

"Unbelievable," Arthur whispered. "Exactly the same number as the EDLS of the key code."

"And here it is again." I grabbed the facsimile copy of the Leningrad Codex and pointed to the beautifully illuminated carpet page on the front cover, its intricate designs interspersed with passages from the text and the Star of David in the center. The most prominent mathematical and geometric feature surrounding the six-pointed star was a series of large round floral motifs. I counted them for Arthur's benefit. "Sixteen gold floral motifs in the Rocío Madonna and sixteen on the illuminated signature page of the Leningrad Codex. So we can add that to the list of things that connect the codex with the Rocío Madonna."

One of the interesting principles of biblical Hebrew theology was that God communicated with His people through the medium of seemingly impossible *meaningful* coincidences,[4] events that inspired not only awe but also serious contemplation aimed at understanding the deep significance of the miracle.

Figure 11.D. The statue of the Madonna of El Rocío near Almonte, Spain. Note the key in the Madonna's right hand and how the Christ child is perfectly centered, an arrangement that can be seen as reflecting the matrix shown in Figure 11.C, in which *Elohim Alef Tav* is centered on *Rocío Madonna*.

Figure 11.E. Image from the illuminated signature page of the Leningrad Codex facsimile edition.

I still wasn't finished. "Now add this to the mix." I had learned that in addition to being able to expand or contract the matrix by exact degrees like those on an ordinary compass, I could also look to the left or right (forward or backward in the text) to see if related information was encrypted at the same equidistance. So with Arthur looking over my shoulder, I simply moved forward in the text (still aligned into thirty-two columns). I let the automatic program do the translating. "A Virgin behold . . . Mary of Bethlehem . . . Jesus Messiah . . . Jesus Messiah."

מ י נ י ל י כ י ן ז ל י ד ח ת ה י כ י נ ח ר מ ש פ ח ת ה
ח י ל ש א ו ל מ ש פ ח ת ה ש ש א ו ל י א ל ה מ ש פ ח ת ה ש מ ע
ש נ י ס ו ע ש ר י ס א ל ף ו מ א ת י ס ב נ י ג ד ל מ ש פ ח ת
צ פ ו ן מ ש פ ח ח ת ה צ פ ו נ י ל ח ג י מ ש פ ח ת ה ח ג י ל ש
י מ ש פ ח ח ת ה ש ו נ י ל א ז נ י מ ש פ ח ת ה א ז נ י ל ע ר י
פ ח ת ה ע ר י ל א ר ו ד מ ש פ ח ת ה ה א ר ו ד י ל א ר א ל י מ
ר ח ת ה א ר א ל י א ל ה מ ש פ ח ת ב נ י ג ד ל פ ק ד י ה ס א
י ס א ל ף ו ח מ ש מ א ו ת ה ב נ י י ה ו ד ה ה ע ר ו א ו נ ן ו י
מ ע ר ו א ו נ ן ב א ר ץ כ נ ע ן ע ו ב נ י י ה ו ד ה ו ד ה ל מ
ח ת ם ל ש ל ה מ ש פ ח ת ה ש ל נ י ל פ ר ץ מ ש פ ח ת ה פ ר צ
ז ר ח מ ש פ ח ת ה ז ר ח י ה י ו ב נ י פ ר ץ ל ח צ ר ן מ
ח ת ה ה צ ר נ י ל ח מ ו ל מ ש פ ח ת ח מ ו ל י א ל ה מ ש פ
י ה ו ד ה ל פ ק ד י ה ס ש ש ה ו ש ב ע י ם ס א ל ף ו ח מ ש ש מ א
ב נ י י ש ש כ ר ל מ ש פ ח ת ס ת ו ל ע מ ש פ ח ת ה ת ו ל ע י
ו ה מ ש פ ח ת ה פ ו נ י ל י ש ו ב מ ש פ ח ת ה י ש ב י ל ש מ
מ ש פ ח ת ה ש מ ר נ י א ל ה מ ש פ ח ת י ש ש כ ר ל פ ק ד י ה
ר ב ע ה ו ש ש י ם ס א ל ף ו ש ל ש מ א ו ת ב נ י ז ב ו ל ן ל מ
ח ת ם ל ס ר ד מ ש פ ח ת ה ס ר ד י ל א ל ו ן מ ש פ ח ת ה א ל

Figure 11.F. Matrix containing encryptions surrounding the *Rocío Madonna* encryption.

I turned and looked at my friend's face, knowing that Arthur was not convinced of the existence of God. He seemed to be struggling for a plausible explanation.

"Timothy, this is all really bizarre. I mean, the legend of the hunter and the Virgin Mary has got to be some sort of allegory. Whatever the truth was behind it has been lost over the centuries. But *someone* knew *something* about the Hebrew Scriptures and their connection with what you're showing me. It's just that the chronology makes no sense."

"I agree. Because we know for certain that the codex existed in its present form and letter sequence well before Alfonso X was born. His Jewish scribes and translators might have made him aware of it, but he couldn't have invented any part of this. Some accounts claim that the discovery of the image on the stump in the thicket occurred as far back as the eighth century. Even among the faithful there's no agreement on when it occurred, only that it apparently became formalized during the reign of Alfonso."

"But why would Jewish scholars reveal to the king of Spain that the Torah was encrypted with information about the Virgin Mary and Bethlehem? And the Son she brought forth, Elohim Alef Tav, 'He who was honored of God'? And all that stuff about Jesus the Messiah? It seems amazing, but it makes no sense for it to be encrypted into the *Hebrew* text."

"Seems counterintuitive, but it's really not at all. You know perfectly well, Arthur, that many Jewish scholars and scribes in Spain at that time had converted to Christianity. And while some may have done so out of convenience or intimidation, others did so very sincerely and for very good reasons."

He took a few steps back and sank into a wing chair.

I swiveled my chair to face him. "I think that in order to find the answer I'm going to have to go deeper into the thicket."

12

The Plot Widens

Italy, May 2015

I could hardly contain my excitement, even after a ten-hour transatlantic flight, as the Boeing 767 began to descend to the Leonardo da Vinci International Airport, the larger of the two airports serving Rome. The pouring rain obscured any view I might have had of the Eternal City, so I glanced over at the third of my six sons. Now twenty-five years old, Abraham sat next to me in the window seat, clutching the backpack of camera gear with which we would document the events we hoped would transpire over the next few weeks.

It was our first visit to Rome, but we weren't coming as tourists. As the plane lumbered toward the gate, I rehearsed in my mind the whirlwind of events that had led to my upcoming meeting with the director of the Vatican Apostolic Library, Archbishop Jean-Louis Bruguès. Besides being the archivist of one of the world's greatest collections of historical texts, the archbishop was perhaps the Roman Catholic Church's most noted theologian. Over the last several years I had met with astrophysicists, ancient-language experts, defense-intelligence analysts, statisticians, geneticists, treasure hunters, and grave robbers, but this would be my first encounter with such an accomplished theologian. And I was looking forward to it.

This visit hadn't been easy to arrange. The esteemed Dead Sea Scrolls scholar

Dr. Eugene Ulrich had put me in touch with the Vatican Embassy in Washington, DC (and graciously offered a few pointers for the process). The embassy sent my formal request for a meeting to the Vatican via a diplomatic pouch, along with formal letters of introduction and references alerting the archbishop to the matter I hoped to discuss with him and perhaps others. A few weeks later I received an official confirmation from Archbishop Carlo Maria Viganò, the Apostolic nuncio in Washington. I was in!

When my son and I landed in Rome, we had a clear idea of whom we needed to see and what we hoped to accomplish. I had peculiar questions for Archbishop Bruguès. I wasn't sure exactly how much about my quixotic quest I would reveal to him or others in the Vatican, but I hoped to learn what I could from him and maybe even see some heretofore undiscovered treasures related to my research in the Hebrew text.

I also hoped he would provide me with a crucial letter of recommendation I needed to secure the cooperation of perhaps the world's oldest and most secretive Christian fraternal organization and to gain access to their vast collection of documents and artifacts related to the Rocío Madonna, a statue of whom I assumed at the time was the Virgin Mary clothed in a beautiful embroidered gown, in the town of Almonte in southern Spain.

For five days Abraham and I tried everything we could do to meet with Archbishop Bruguès. One thing after another forced us to reschedule: Pope Francis saying Mass in Saint Peter's Square, increased security over terrorist threats, a national holiday, and then confusion with the Swiss Guards at the Vatican gates. Eventually, we were told that the only possible time to meet would be a week later.

We *were* in Rome, after all, so my son and I took in the splendors of the Eternal City, wandering the ancient streets and alleyways, lingering in the May sunshine at sidewalk cafés, nosing into shops and market stalls, and of course exploring the magnificent ancient ruins, museums, and cathedrals. We saved our tour of the Vatican museums and Saint Peter's Basilica for last. While Abraham took countless photos and vast amounts of video, I gazed around with a mixture of awe and admiration. To be standing in the midst of a place so rich with the masterworks of art and culture, so deeply rooted in history and tradition, so firmly seated atop centuries of power and influence made it seem impossible that the report of my discoveries in an ancient Hebrew codex would make any real difference to the guardians of such an imposing institution. In any case, it seemed likely to be a moot point, as our prospects for an audience with the archbishop now hung by a thread.

There seemed to be little or nothing we could do about it, however. We had acquired no letter of recommendation, and our plans so far had come to naught. After five days in Rome, we hopped a flight to Seville, Spain, the capital city of the province of Andalusia, and the next morning we took a bus eighty kilometers southwest to El Rocío, a sprawling village of sandy, unpaved roads traversed by more horses and wagons than cars or buses. Under a blazing sun we dragged our luggage and photography equipment down a dusty street. Having no clue as to how we were going to proceed, we spied a local real estate office. There we did our best to communicate to the proprietor and his companions that we had come from the United States and hoped to meet with the Primordial Order of the Virgin of El Rocío. We told them we had something miraculous to show them and many questions to ask them.

After a few minutes of head scratching and funny looks, someone made a phone call and told us to wait on the front porch. Within fifteen minutes a car pulled up and a woman emerged. She spoke English with an unmistakable German accent.

"Hello, I will help you if I can. My name is Marina."

I told Marina the purpose of our visit. She was delighted. In halting English, she told us she loved history and thought our story of finding the name of the Rocío Madonna in the book of Genesis was fascinating. Strangely, she said that fact did not surprise her, adding that she believed God had brought us together. She agreed to help us but had only a half hour to spare that morning from her job working with special-needs children. She also warned that arranging a meeting with the Primordial brotherhood would be difficult.

"They are very closed," she said. "They don't admit people from the outside." She assured us, however, that she "knew people who knew people" and, if we could be patient, she might succeed in arranging a meeting for us. She worried, though, that her limited ability to translate English to Spanish might pose an obstacle.

Marina had to return to work, but she said that as soon as we were settled at our hotel we must compose an e-mail explaining our discoveries and especially how they related to the Rocío Madonna. She would then forward the e-mail to her brother in South Africa, who spoke perfect English. She could then call him so he could explain everything to her in German, which would give her a much better understanding of the situation. Then she could convey our request in Spanish to her work partner Raphael. He would then serve as our spokesman if arrangements could be made to meet with the brotherhood. Any questions we had would be handled the same way.

We agreed to the plan without hesitation and for the next three days negotiated possible times and circumstances for a meeting with some unnamed persons at the brotherhood headquarters in Almonte. Any sensible conference would of course require the attendance of Marina and Raphael, both of whom were swamped with work responsibilities as the busy week of the pilgrimage to the Rocío Madonna approached. We were scheduled to fly back to Rome in time to make a rescheduled appointment with Archbishop Bruguès at the Vatican Library, so our window of opportunity was closing fast. Finally, a time was set that gave us just enough time to catch our flight to Rome.

The morning of the meeting Marina came to our hotel and informed us there was a scheduling snag and she wasn't sure when or even if another meeting could be arranged. It was a crushing disappointment, and she was clearly upset herself. We thanked her for her efforts and tried to reassure her that all was not lost, that we would try to set up an e-mail line of communication and do what we could from a distance. Dejected, we said our good-byes, and Abraham and I packed up our things, checked out of the hotel, and hurried to the bus stop.

As we waited in the shelter for the morning bus to Seville, we tried to tell ourselves that our trip had not been a total bust. We had certainly enjoyed the beauty of the village, which lay at the edge of a beautiful lake and marshland that were part of the expansive Doñana National Park. Beautiful Andalusian horses grazed freely on the lush grasslands.

On the first day of our visit, just after meeting Marina, we had gone to the Chapel of the Virgin and seen its stunning rococo altar featuring the statue of the Madonna. There I saw firsthand what I had scrutinized and studied for nearly a year.

We spent hours in the chapel taking photographs and video and closely examining what we had previously seen only in the scant images available from public sources. We took note of all of the intriguing characteristics of the chapel and altarpiece that had caught my attention when I first discovered the *Rocío Madonna* encryption inside the key-code matrix in Genesis 30. All this provided some consolation but little enough compared to what I had hoped to accomplish here.

We boarded the bus and said good-bye to El Rocío. At least I had spent some quality time with my son, who would soon be starting graduate studies in Colorado far from home. As the bus circled the block and nosed onto the main road to Seville, my cell phone, which had been practically useless throughout our travels, started ringing inside my briefcase. I thought it would be my wife calling from the States. After some fumbling, I pulled it out and answered.

It wasn't my wife.

"Hello, Timothy, this is Marina. Where are you?"

"We're on the bus headed to Seville. We have to catch a flight to Rome."

"No, no, you must come back. I have the meeting for you tomorrow at twelve. You must be there. It is now arranged."

"But we will miss our return flight from Rome if we stay."

"You must stay," Marina insisted. "The person you must talk to will be there. He is the one who knows everything."

I told her we would come back. Then I jumped up from my seat and called to the driver to stop the bus. Abraham and I grabbed our luggage, exited onto the highway at the edge of town, and began trudging back into El Rocío, feeling the curious stares of the driver and passengers as the bus moved off without us. We checked back into our hotel, and my son soon managed to book the only flight from Seville that would put us in Rome in time to make our return flight to the States. The Vatican Library was off. All our bets were now placed on our meeting with the brotherhood.

At promptly 11:00 the next morning, Marina and Raphael picked us up and we headed off to Almonte. On the short drive we rehearsed everything with them until they were confident everyone was on the same page. Arriving at the brotherhood headquarters, where the massive pine doors of the Renaissance structure appeared hundreds of years older than the building itself, we were greeted by an attendant and asked to wait in the antechamber.

Soon a man, considerably younger than I'd expected, entered and greeted us warmly. Marina offered introductions all around. Manuel was the chief historian and archivist for the Primordial Order of the Virgin of El Rocío. He was working on his doctoral thesis on the history and tradition of the Rocío Madonna. Raphael explained in Spanish the purpose of our visit to Manuel and his staff. I understood virtually nothing until Manuel's face registered shock and he asked Raphael to repeat something. I inferred it was to make sure he had heard it correctly.

Manuel then escorted everyone into his private office and asked an attendant to supply chairs for us all. He shut the door and apparently asked Raphael to repeat his explanation once again. Animated conversation ensued between Manuel and Raphael, with Raphael turning occasionally to Marina for clarification in Spanish and Marina turning for support from me in English. At some point during this process, I committed a faux pas. In the course of asking a question about the legend of the miraculous appearance of the Virgin to the hunter in the thicket, I referred to her as the Virgin Mary.

Manuel shook his head. "Not the Virgin Maria," he said rather sternly. "The Virgin Rocío." The others in the room nodded solemnly. I apologized and we moved on.

I would learn later that the Virgin of Rocío was never referred to in any of the fraternity's public or private publications *exclusively* as the Virgin Mary. The Primordial brotherhood considers her identity and tradition to be entirely unique and separate from all other Marian devotions.

Soon I was showing Manuel, the historian of the brotherhood, the Genesis 30 matrix referring to the Rocío Madonna on my laptop. I stood behind him, looking over his shoulder, as he carefully traced his finger from bottom to top, following the letters that spelled *Madonna* (מדונה) in Hebrew and then slowly and carefully tracing from top to bottom the letters that spelled *Rocío* (רוזיו).

Well, I thought, *it's obvious he can read Hebrew.*

After a few moments he shook his head from side to side in what seemed like a mix of disbelief and recognition. Suddenly he stood and strode from the room without another word. His abrupt departure surprised us, but we didn't have time to comment on it before he returned with a computer flash drive in hand. He plugged it into his computer on the desk, clicked the mouse, and then beckoned me to look over his shoulder.

It was my turn to be surprised. On the screen were magnified images of the sunburst motifs that adorn the statue of the Virgin of El Rocío (see Figure 11.D). Having previously seen only photographs of these features (and, of course, having viewed the actual statue from a distance just days before), I had never been able to see that engraved in the iris of each medallion was a tiny symbol (see Figures 12.A through 12.D). Manuel said the same symbols had been embroidered on the trim of the succession of gowns that had adorned the wooden statue over the centuries. Most important, they were the original symbols that, according to legend, adorned the Virgin's garment when she appeared to the hunter atop the tree stump in the thicket.

I knew these symbols reflected ancient Christian traditions that associated the Virgin Mary with the ark of the covenant (Moses placed the words of God inside the ark, and her womb sheltered the incarnate "Word of God"). All the symbols were related to the oldest known Marian litanies (going as far back as the fourth or fifth century AD) and had intertwined throughout European history with crypto-Judaism, whereby Jews secretly practiced their faith while publicly professing conversion to Christianity. The presence of these secret Jews is particularly well documented in Spain as a result of the 1391 Jewish pogroms and their persecution and expulsion by Ferdinand and Isabella in 1492.

In order to facilitate this subterfuge and prevent the destruction of the objects of their devotion, especially Torah scrolls and books, many Jewish communities converted their synagogues to Christian chapels. In the process it was common to remove the Torah ark from its niche and replace it with a wooden statue of the Virgin Mary. Over the years these statues became extravagantly decorated, and the synagogues were modified, renovated, and slowly transformed as many descendants of those persecuted Jews assimilated into the fabric of Catholic culture.

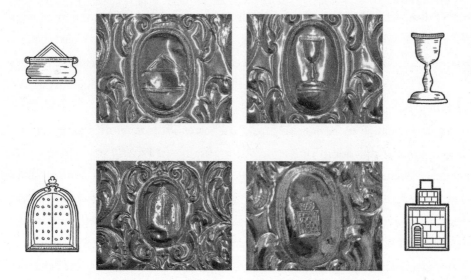

Figure 12.A. Four of the sixteen icons on the Rocío Madonna statue depicting (clockwise from top left) the ark of the covenant, the Grail Chalice, the Tower of David, and the Torah ark.

Figure 12.C. Icons on the Rocío Madonna statue depicting (clockwise from top left) a fountain, a mirror, a well, and a monstrance (vessel for consecrated bread or a sacred relic).

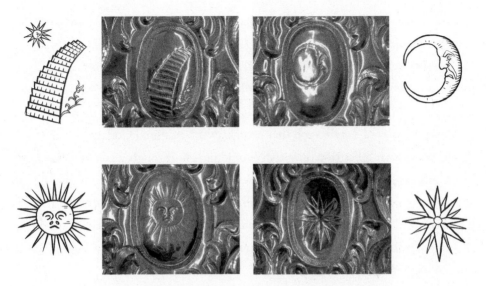

Figure 12.B. Icons on the Rocío Madonna statue depicting (clockwise from top left) a staircase or ladder of sixteen steps, a crescent moon, a sixteen-pointed "morning star," and a sun.

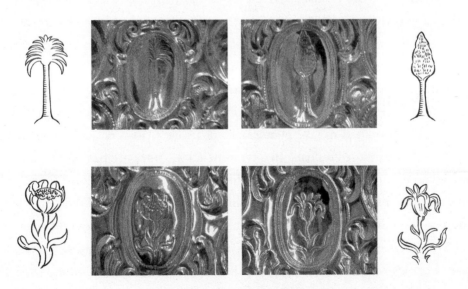

Figure 12.D. Icons on the Rocío Madonna statue depicting (clockwise from top left) a palm tree, a cypress tree, a lily, and a rose.

But what would those crypto-Jews have done with their Torah scrolls and *chu-mashim* (printed versions of the Torah)? Certainly many were lost or destroyed, but surely many *conversos* (as Jewish converts to the Catholic Church were called) preserved and hid their precious artifacts. What ancient treasures might still be hidden in churches and shrines around the globe? Could one or more of them contain a yet-to-be-discovered Torah scroll that predates the Leningrad Codex? Where would they conceal such relics to ensure they would be safe through waves of persecution in a Catholic-dominated Europe? Where would they put them where they might still retain a position of honor and symbolic continuity? What sort of ritual and devotion would they devise to ensure that no one in Catholic society would dream of molesting the artifacts? (These questions help explain my consuming interest in finding such artifacts.)

I really had nothing to lose at this point, so I reached into the pocket of my computer case, pulled out my own flash drive, and asked Manuel if I could copy the sixteen images. To my surprise, he agreed. While the images were being transferred I looked over at Abraham, my third son, born in a blizzard twenty-five years ago in the tiny cabin in the Canadian wilderness where in many ways this quest had begun. He smiled knowingly as he stood in the corner of the room snapping photographs, trying to be as discreet as possible. Both of us were certain we were in the right place at the right time, no matter how we'd stumbled into it. Nothing had worked out the way we planned, and yet it had all worked out perfectly.

After our meetings we were provided with a tour of the extensive museum and library and permitted to take photographs of artifacts, artwork, and manuscripts that would later prove invaluable in our research. I was intrigued by the vast number of genealogical records stored in the archives. The brotherhood seemed fixated on the ancestral lineage of its members, which traced back to the Middle Ages and beyond. This meticulous attention to bloodlines turned out to be one of the primary tasks of the archivist and his staff. I was told that applications for admission into any of the branches of brotherhoods could take years, even decades, to process.

I gathered that Manuel and his staff had recently come to suspect that a hidden mystery was attached to the tradition for which their generation now served as primary caretaker. That may have been what inspired their recent cataloging of records and items that had not been looked at for centuries. It also resulted in a digital photographic inventory of the Rocío Madonna statue and her associated accoutrements. Apparently that's when the sixteen engraved symbols were discovered and photographed by the current staff, which initiated a search for more information concerning their provenance.

When Manuel saw *Rocío Madonna* encoded plainly in Genesis 30, precisely intersecting with the phrase "Her womb opened, and she conceived and brought forth a son," he connected the words—and the fact that sixteen was the equidistant letter skip that revealed the key code in the first place—with the sixteen symbols. Manuel and his staff had often wondered why there was so much emphasis on the number sixteen in the iconography surrounding the Virgin of El Rocío. I only wished I had more time and the ability to speak Spanish so I could cover more ground with Manuel.

The meeting ended much too quickly, but we were invited to return soon and with much more enthusiasm than mere courtesy would have suggested. With every step I took down the cobblestone street and away from the archive, the more convinced I became that not only was this ancient brotherhood in possession of a treasure the world knew nothing about, but its current stewards were unaware of it as well.

Even though Manuel made the undeniable connection between the *Rocío Madonna* encryption in Genesis 30 and the sixteen tiny symbols engraved on the sixteen golden sunbursts that adorned the statue of the Virgin, he and his colleagues admitted they were unable to interpret their full meaning and significance. They were apparently in possession of some early document that spoke of sixteen symbols embroidered on the hem of the garment of the Virgin when she appeared to the hunter in the thicket, but that was all they knew—or at least all they were telling me.

When I'd told them the number sixteen had unlocked the key code where the *Rocío Madonna* encryption was discovered, they were not only mystified but truly excited. That's the reason Manuel allowed me to copy the photographs. He was stunned at the bizarre synchronicity of Abe and me showing up with our discovery, right on the heels of his own discovery.

In the Tomb of a King

We thanked Marina and Raphael warmly for all their crucial assistance as they let us off at the bus station in Almonte. From there we planned to dash to Seville, hop a flight to Rome the next morning, and make our connecting flight to the United States.

When we arrived in Seville, there was no question, however, as to how we would spend the rest of the afternoon. We had to figure out some way to get into the royal chapel in the Seville Cathedral. Here was the tomb of Alfonso X, king of Castile who, in the thirteenth century, was supposedly the first Spanish monarch to take the Virgin of El Rocío under his wing. Contrary to some of our previous assumptions, we knew now that the wise king by no means invented the legend of the Rocío Madonna. In fact, given the well-documented details of his life and reign, we wondered if this legend and devotion were really all that important to him. But there are few things in life that reveal more about people's deepest beliefs than their funeral and burial, particularly in the case of royalty, who are in a position to make certain that their last earthly wishes are carried out. It's their last chance to make a statement.

The guard at the massive iron gate in Seville held up a hand. *"No. Usted no puede entrar,"* he said. Even I could understand that much Spanish, but the guard continued to make certain Abe and I got the message. *"No hay visitantes. Sólo para la oración."* Why would they pay a guy to stand there all day just to tell people they couldn't go into the royal chapel? Why not just lock the gate and be done with it?

Abe and I made a long circuit around the largest cathedral in the world as we contemplated the obvious loophole in "No visitors, only prayer." A half hour later we arrived at the entrance once again, only to discover that a new guard had replaced our nemesis. Without explaining his plan to me, Abe stashed his camera in his pack and headed to the gate with his head lowered.

"Hemos venido a orar," he said solemnly, putting his hand on his chest as if to indicate some deep inner turmoil. The new gatekeeper, a man in his midsixties, pointed to me. *"Mi padre,"* Abe responded. I inferred that my role was somehow related to Abe's troubled heart. Was I sick? Whatever the case, I had little time to get into character, but the gatekeeper acquiesced as if my son had uttered the secret password.

Inside the chapel, Abe and I knelt in the front pew. To our left, in the shadows, was the towering marble tomb of Alfonso X of Castile. Some twenty feet in front of us lay the lavishly embellished, silver-clad altar that was the centerpiece of the royal chapel of the Spanish monarchy, positioned in the heart of the massive cathedral. In the dim candlelight we strained to make out the iconographical details that adorned this stunning work of symbolic art. Behind and beside us were iron-gated burial niches bedecked with silver and gold accoutrements and glittering regalia befitting royalty. Our minder hovered in the doorway, eyeing us suspiciously.

For several frustrating minutes we knelt there, trapped by our own ruse, unable to closely examine any revealing particulars the Spanish kings may have left for us. Just as I was wondering how much trouble we'd get ourselves into by approaching the tomb for a closer look, the guard, apparently distracted by a commotion outside, suddenly disappeared, leaving us momentarily alone in the medieval chamber.

"Get out the camera," I whispered.

"No way. It's not going to work. There's not enough light, and he'll be back any second."

"Let's just look. We're paying our last respects, so we need to get as close as we can and quickly!"

We dashed for the wrought-iron barrier that served to keep anyone from getting too close to the altar. The flames of the candles flanking the altar flickered in the drafty cavern, causing the elaborate silverwork to glimmer. We had no more than thirty seconds to absorb the details before the guard reappeared in the doorway. He headed straight for us and, without saying a word, gruffly escorted us out the door and back into the bustling streets of Seville.

"Did you see what I saw?" I asked as soon as we were out of earshot.

"Yes. Yes, I think so. What did you see?"

"No, you first."

"Okay, well, I was concentrating on the top and the front. The scenes were in relief in exactly the same form as the sixteen gold Rocío Madonna symbols. They were all narrative panels, but I couldn't see the sides. The central panel was definitely the Virgin appearing to someone. A knight or a king on their knees."

"Yeah, I saw all that. Did you see any of the other iconography?"

"Some. Did you?"

"Yes, but they were all integrated into the narrative scenes. They were story panels, just like a medieval tapestry. But I couldn't see the side panels either. Or the back."

"It's so weird," Abe mused. "The very central focus of the medieval Spanish monarchy's religious devotion, and they're depicting a Marian apparition."

"I know it seems really crazy. If you consider their wide-ranging interests and achievements and all the endless complexities of managing an empire, not to mention a library containing the most important literary, scientific, and scriptural manuscripts of the day, the fact that the royal tomb and chapel give such prominence to Marian apparitions means they must have felt it was supremely important."

"Yet the Spanish historians hardly mention the connection."

"Right. They say only in passing that many monarchs at the time were devotees of the Virgin Mary but never get specific about it. You can go on the Internet and find close-up pictures of nearly everything in the cathedral, but not in the royal chapel, and especially not the central altar or any of the smaller side altars, for that matter. Add this to everything we learned in Almonte this morning, and it starts to look like something is being covered up."

"No," Abe countered. "Not *is* being covered up. *Was* being covered up. Manuel turned over those photographs to us. He's not trying to hide anything. After we showed him the key code, I think he wants to know what this is all about as much as we do."

"That's true. Good point."

The sun was beginning to set as Abe and I strolled toward the Guadalquivir River, comparing notes and observations, trying to make sense of what we'd seen. We crossed the Triana Bridge just as crowds were coming out to enjoy the beautiful evening. Andalusians of all ages mingled on the sidewalks and in cafés as we chose a street-side table for a last local meal that always began with a complimentary bowl of plump green olives brought in daily from the endless groves between Seville and El Rocío. Amid the cheerful chatter of Spanish voices we continued our deliberations, interrupted only by the arrival of the street musicians who solicited a spare euro or two in exchange for a passionate flamenco ballad, incomprehensible to me but for the hauntingly familiar sense of unspeakable sadness.

On that last night of our adventure the focus of our musings wandered from one topic to the next but finally came to rest on a particular theme, a sort of rendezvous point for all things connected to the Rocío Madonna. For in the days leading up to our encounter with the Primordial brotherhood, Abe and I had not been wasting our time. We'd put ourselves through a crash course on the Virgin of El Rocío tradition and Marian devotion in general. We visited dozens of chapels and cathedrals in Rome and Seville, each dedicated to the Virgin Mary and each with its own unique tradition.

As I've noted before, I am not Roman Catholic, although my early years as a Christian were spent in the Catholic faith. And I am by no means a Marian devotee myself, but I acknowledge how important these various traditions are to millions worldwide and have since discovered that something of profound importance lies hidden behind the modern rituals and pilgrimages, something very intentionally cloaked in a garb calculated to be inviolate to the persecutions of the Roman Church, particularly during the dark days of the Inquisition.

Nearly all of these traditions were spawned by a miraculous encounter with a feminine personage, believed of course to be Mary the Virgin Mother of Jesus Christ. But an entirely separate common thread connected the Virgin of El Rocío tradition, which was by far the oldest, with a handful of other unique traditions that depict the Virgin as a woman whose identity is far more complex than that of simply Mary, the Virgin Mother.

The origin for these traditions and the symbolic imagery employed to convey the mystery of what came to be called the *Theotokos* ("God bearer") can be traced back to the apocalypse of John in Revelation, the last book of the Bible. This had been observed by theologians and art historians, but we were now confronted with evidence that this drama had begun long before the revelation John received on the island of Patmos.

And there appeared a great wonder in heaven; a woman clothed with the sun, and the moon under her feet, and upon her head a crown of twelve stars: and she being with child cried, travailing in birth, and pained to be delivered. And there appeared another wonder in heaven; and behold a great red dragon, having seven heads and ten horns, and seven crowns upon his heads. And his tail drew the third part of the stars of heaven, and did cast them to the earth: and the dragon stood before the woman which was ready to be delivered, for to devour her child as soon as it was born. And she brought forth a man child, who was to rule all nations with a rod of iron: and her child was caught up unto God, and to his throne. And the woman fled into the wilderness, where she hath a place prepared of God, that they should feed her there a thousand two hundred and threescore days.[1]

As my son and I made our way back to our hotel on the east bank of the Guadalquivir, we agreed that the Lady of Rocío—the "Woman Clothed with the Sun," this "Woman of the Apocalypse"—was the one we'd been seeking. For it was becoming clearer by the hour that the Rocío Madonna tradition and the distinct symbolism attached to her legend represented an intersection of not only many fascinating historical threads but also all things associated with the ark of the covenant, the repository for the Word of God.

The Virgin Mary's womb was of course, literally, the protective repository for Jesus Christ, the Word of God. She kept Him safe and hidden until the time arrived for Him to speak to the house of Israel. The *Rocío Madonna* encryption in the book of Genesis expressly states that "her womb opened, and she conceived and brought forth a son," and it depicts her holding "Elohim Alpha Omega."

The Primordial Order of the Virgin of El Rocío had, in litany and ceremony, treated the wooden statue as if it were the very ark of the covenant for so many hundreds of years that they were not sure themselves exactly when—and precisely why—they were doing this. But the unique ritual and symbolism had continued nonetheless, a familiar scenario to be sure, and one that I'd learned not to underestimate for its uncanny ability to safeguard precious kernels of historical truth.

My son and I came to Andalusia with the far-fetched notion that we might uncover merely a pristine fragment of ancient Scripture. We left with the profound intuition that we were on course to uncover something far greater.

Figure 12.E. Artist's depiction of the "Woman Clothed with
the Sun" and the great red dragon of Revelation 12.

PART IV

SIGNS AND WARNINGS

13

Led Every Step of the Way

Cape Hatteras National Seashore is a seventy-mile-long sliver of sand strung precariously along the Atlantic coast of North Carolina. It is one of the most vulnerable inhabited places in North America, absorbing the brunt of the regular seasonal hurricanes that gather fury over Caribbean waters before unleashing their wrath on the Eastern Seaboard. Most of the beachfront is wild and undeveloped.

This is where the two great basins of the East Coast meet and the cold waters of the Labrador Current collide with the warm waters of the Gulf Stream. The shallow sandbars heaved up by this unrelenting turbulence form the treacherous Diamond Shoals, where hundreds of shipwrecks lie in what is known as the Graveyard of the Atlantic. Not far from the historic Cape Hatteras Lighthouse, which flashes out its ceaseless warning to seafarers, a close family friend has a little cottage.

There, on an uncommonly warm autumn morning, I ventured onto a long stretch of deserted beach to gather my thoughts. I like being on the extreme edge of the continent, where I can watch the first rays of the morning sun light up the eastern horizon, where the sound of gulls and wind and waves can wash my mind clear of all the distractions of this fast-paced, high-tech world. On that particular morning I had a great many distractions to clear away and a multitude of thoughts to gather.

Fifteen years earlier I could have tucked away the strange coincidence I'd discovered in the book of Genesis as a charming curiosity, an entertaining story to be passed on to my children and grandchildren, perhaps. But it was too late for that now. My incessant curiosity had uncovered far more than I ever could have imagined, more than the remarkable accuracy of the ancient text, more than the deep significance of the Bible's accounts and narratives, more than the understanding that the words and letters of the Bible were not only carefully preserved but also precisely arranged. I believed that my strange experience twenty-five years earlier in the Canadian Rockies was connected with something tangible in the Old Testament. And I knew that as much as I had learned of God and His Word already, there was much I had yet to explore.

I sensed that God was speaking not only in the canon of Scripture but also in new ways that, like the lighthouse towering nearby, were flashing out a warning both timely and timeless. As if all that didn't give me enough to think about as I walked that vulnerable stretch of sand, I now had to grapple with something else I'd just learned, something that added still more layers of wonder and meaning to everything I had unearthed to date.

GRANDFATHER'S WARDROBE

Before I elaborate on what was causing me even deeper fascination with the Hebrew text, I want to share one more dream.

Years earlier I had a vivid dream in which I was visited by my maternal grandfather. His name was Joseph Zangla. As a child I understood my mother's father was Italian. This was logical enough, as he had arrived in the United States in the 1920s from Naples via the busy gateway of Ellis Island, New York. While he was in the Italian army during World War I, he had been captured and forced to spend much of the war in a German prison camp in Austria.

In the early eighties, not long before my grandfather's death, I received a large amount of genealogical information from an uncle regarding my Smith and Marlow ancestors, which sparked my interest in family history and prompted me to pursue my matriarchal lineage as well. I was fortunate in those pre-Internet days to live within minutes of the National Archives in Washington, DC. There I spent many hours trying to sort out (with the assistance of the helpful staff) Grandfather

Joseph's somewhat confusing heritage. What follows is a near-verbatim account taken from my journal entry for January 16, 1992, when I had a dream about my grandfather.

> Last night in a dream I was visited by my grandfather Joseph (my mother's father). He gave me a large book and beckoned me to open it and look at the pictures. The first showed my grandfather riding a horse-drawn cart of his own design along a beautiful stretch of beach. As I looked at the picture the scene came to life, and I seemed to enter into it. Grandfather's horse and cart gleamed in the warm sun, and I could sense his youthful exhilaration as he sped by.
>
> A moment came in my dream when I was standing in Grandfather Joseph's house. . . .
>
> I found myself holding a beautiful purple band or sash, some three or four inches wide and nearly ten feet long. It was embroidered with symbols stitched in gold thread that repeated every foot or so. I understood that I was preparing the wardrobe for transportation by performing the ceremonial sealing of its doors with the purple sash. My grandfather explained to me that his father had given him the sash and that his father had also received it from his father, and so on through many generations. He explained that it was not just a birthright and that each generation had to be instructed in its proper handling.
>
> Having only been in a synagogue a few times in my life, I assumed that what I took to be a wardrobe contained robes or clothing of some sort, but my grandfather never intimated that to me. [Note: It was some years later that I realized the wardrobe was *Aron Kodesh,* or the Torah ark]. Once I used the purple band to seal the doors of the cabinet, I asked Grandfather Joseph if I could have a band of my own. He was very pleased with my request and produced a beautiful purple one embroidered with the same curious golden symbols. He walked toward me and extended his gift, but no sooner had I reached out to take it than the dream suddenly ended and I found myself lying wide awake in my bed.

This dream ignited my curiosity about my grandfather's heredity. It also prepared me for the recent discovery (1983) that a relative of my grandfather who now lived in the United States was a Jewish rabbi. When I got in touch with him, he told me that as far as he knew, the Zanglas had lived in Sicily for hundreds of years (if not longer), moving in and out of hiding as the winds of Jewish persecution shifted across Europe. Some families converted to Roman Catholicism and in time lost touch with their Jewish origins, while others clung to their beliefs and traditions, sometimes openly, sometimes secretly.

I probed my distant cousin about the family name, Zangla, but he was unable to give me any insight, admitting that it was a mystery to him as well. As I pursued the matter further, I confirmed that the name had no Latin origins, but neither did it seem to have Jewish roots, at least not among the Sephardim; that is, Jews of Spanish or Portuguese origin.

My beach walk on Cape Hatteras neared its end. I passed the lighthouse and headed slowly back to the cottage. The tide had gone out, leaving crystal-clear saltwater trapped in shallow pools along the way. I stood at the edge of one of these for a moment, gazing briefly at my own reflection. Then a thought crossed my mind—and I wondered how a rabbi and a native Hebrew speaker like my cousin could have missed something so obvious.

THE GREATEST TREASURE

Back at my computer, I entered my grandfather's surname in the search field of my decryption program. The Hebrew spelling of the name is straightforward, yet it did not appear in the text, at least not as I knew it. After an hour or so at my task, I was looking at an example of a common scribal trick called mirror writing. Applying it to my grandfather's name, I found that *Zangla* spelled backward is the Hebrew phrase "the treasure ark," or "highest treasure cabinet." In all the books of the Hebrew Bible the phrase is used only in the book of Esther and is usually translated as "the treasuries."

It seems reasonable to assume that at some point, in order to conceal the Jewish origins of his name, my grandfather's family simply let it stand from left to right as it would appear in Spanish or Latin, thus producing *Zangla*. It was a subterfuge that would have succeeded in the Roman Empire and the medieval world, where few Gentiles, even among the literate, could read Hebrew. This would explain why the name had no apparent source among Italian or Jewish names and was likely never a surname at all in the conventional sense.

It also rather strikingly underscored what I had understood my grandfather to be showing me in my dream, for his surname literally meant "the treasure ark" or "highest treasure cabinet." In the dream, my grandfather showed me a royal band that was used to seal and unseal the doors to the Torah cabinet. Naturally, like anyone else, I suppose, I wanted access to the treasure cabinet where the words of God were preserved and protected. In the dream, Grandfather made it clear, however, that regardless of my ancestry, I did not have the unrestricted privilege to open and close the doors of the treasury, for only by faith and instruction was this honor granted.

I also intuited that in the dream I was standing in for anyone and everyone who sought to open the treasure ark. In fact, this sense that I was a representative for others was the same feeling I had in many of my dreams and spiritual encounters.

This strange discovery at this late stage compelled me to go back over everything I'd discovered. Could the origins of my maternal grandfather's surname somehow connect thematically to the key code? Whatever connection my ancestors may have had to the king's treasuries in the past had been lost along the way. My only recourse seemed to be further investigation of the Hebrew Bible.

So I began searching again and returned to the encryption that was perhaps the most precise reference in the text to a time in history. It was the only specific day, month, and year that was positively encrypted in the Hebrew Bible from the time the Gregorian calendar was reconciled with the Hebrew calendar in AD 1752 to the present: my birth date ("on the twenty-first day of February 1960"), preceded by the sign of the double nails (vav vav). I had noticed previously how the vav vav "double nail sign" directly preceded or followed some of the most noteworthy encryptions. This is, of course, the symbolism used in the *Timotheus* chiasmus, and it is coincidentally a sign and symbol used in many esoteric ritual ceremonies. So naturally I checked to see if anything was written or encoded in the matrix that was related to what my grandfather seemed to be telling me in my dream.

There, in Joshua 3:17, in perfect symmetrical balance across the code containing my birthdate was the unmistakable phrase "the priests that carry the ark."

Figure 13.A. Vertical, bottom to top: *23/Sh'vat/5720* ("on the twenty-first day of February 1960").[1] Horizontal, right to left: "the priests that carry the ark."

Grandfather Zangla's appearance in a dream with a Torah ark was obviously intriguing to me, whereas it might seem meaningless to most other people. But the strange intersection of my dream, my grandfather's name, and the Hebrew Bible seemed not just to stretch but to shatter the limits of probability.

THE HIDDEN QUEEN

Because of this connection to my newly discovered Jewish grandfather, I was drawn to the book of Esther and the tale of the exiled Jewish girl who found herself caught up in something far beyond her experience and understanding, leaving her to act the best way she knew how. In that, I certainly identified with her. But now, of course, I had the added consideration of my grandfather's name appearing in the text of Esther. Her story, commemorated every year by the Feast of Purim, has always been considered unique by many rabbis and Bible scholars who saw in it strange parallels with events in the twentieth century, particularly the Holocaust and the Nuremberg war-crime trials.[2]

The story takes place during or soon after the Jewish exile in Babylon (605–536 BC). On the surface it's about a beautiful Jewish girl, Hadassah, orphaned as a child, who becomes Esther, queen of the vast Persian Empire. (Her husband, King Ahasuerus, knows nothing of Esther's Jewish heritage.) One of the kingdom's highest officials, a man named Haman who hates the Jewish people, obtains the king's permission to launch a "final solution" against the Jews throughout the Persian Empire. But Esther, with the help of her uncle, Mordecai, thwarts Haman's terrible plan.

Using what I had learned from the key code and all the other encrypted information to date, I pored over the book of Esther. It would prove to be the meeting place of all my dreams and visions, of all my peculiar historical discoveries, and of all the remarkable encryptions I'd uncovered in the Hebrew Bible. Though God is never explicitly mentioned in the book of Esther, it seemed to me so much that had been hidden was now being revealed for me, and the name and sign of Elohim Alef Tav, the crucified Messiah, in the text of the thousand-year-old Leningrad Codex, was leading me every step of the way.

No Time for Silence

Once Esther became queen to Ahaseurus, also known as Xerxes, she lived a sheltered and pampered life in the palace. Even Mordecai, her uncle, had to communicate by sending messages to her chamber. Mordecai learned of Haman's plan to exterminate the Jews throughout the empire while Esther remained blissfully ignorant of the danger. Eventually, however, Mordecai sent word to Esther of Haman's plot, urging her to go to the king, reveal herself to be a Jew, and plead with him to stop the impending slaughter of her people.

But there was a problem. Even though Esther was queen, she could not simply enter the king's throne room and have a conversation with him. Persian society was highly structured, with strict protocols that governed the way they lived their lives and ran their country. Anyone, including Esther, who came to the king without being summoned took the chance of embarrassing the king or angering him. In such a case, if the king did not ceremonially extend his scepter to the visitor, the consequence would be death.

Even Esther couldn't count on the king inviting her to see him. In fact, a month had passed since the last time she had been summoned into his presence, and there was no way to tell when, or even if, the king would send for her again. When Esther sent a messenger to her uncle to explain all this, Mordecai turned up the pressure on her to act anyway.

> Do not think to yourself that in the king's palace you will escape any more than all the other Jews. For if you keep silent at this time, relief and deliverance will rise for the Jews from another place, but you and your father's house will perish. And who knows whether you have not come to the kingdom for such a time as this?[3]

Esther's response rings through the centuries, embodying her courage and willingness to sacrifice her own life for the sake of her people. She sent this answer to Mordecai:

Go, gather all the Jews to be found in Susa, and hold a fast on my behalf, and do not eat or drink for three days, night or day. I and my young women will also fast as you do. Then I will go to the king, though it is against the law, and if I perish, I perish.[4]

It was the moment when a star arose in the east, the instant when the hidden was revealed, when the decision was made that would bring deliverance for many on the brink of extinction. I find it inexpressibly inspiring.

But there was more waiting for me in that passage. Encoded over those very verses at an EDLS of twenty-nine is "Timothy vav vav"; that is, "honored of God" followed by the sign of the double nails. Also appearing in the same matrix is my grandfather Joseph's surname as *Zangla* (from left to right) and "the treasure cabinet" (right to left).

ON THE THIRD DAY

The entire Purim drama revolves around the ultimate showdown between those who have faith in the God of Israel, though God remains hidden throughout, and those who despise and oppose God's people. It's a complex plot and difficult to summarize, but Esther did go to the king and enter his throne room without a royal invitation. He extended his scepter to her, a sign of his favor that spared her life. Once she made it past that obstacle, Esther followed a careful and intricate strategy. She invited the king and his ruthless advisor Haman to a banquet that she would host later that day. The king agreed to attend. Then at that first banquet, she extended a *second* invitation to the king and Haman for a banquet the next day, which was also accepted.

In between the two banquets, something occurred that Esther could not have foreseen or arranged. The king, after suffering a bout of insomnia, had the royal records read to him that night, which included an account of the heroic actions of Mordecai, who once had saved the king from an assassination attempt. When the king found out that Mordecai had never been rewarded, he summoned Haman and asked how the king should reward someone who deserves great honor. Haman, thinking the king meant to honor him, proposed lavish rewards, only to have the king order that such honors be extended to Mordecai, whom Haman had secretly planned to hang that very day.

While Haman was still fuming with hatred and frustration, he attended Esther's second banquet. There Esther revealed her Jewish identity to the king, telling him that she, along with her people, faced annihilation and that Haman was responsible. Haman begged for mercy, but the king ordered him hanged, which he was, on the very gallows he had built for Mordecai.

Even then, the story doesn't end. It was too late to reverse the proclamation ordering the destruction of the Jews, but when Esther pressed her case, the king agreed to a plan. A new proclamation would be issued allowing the Jews to arm and defend themselves and to confiscate the property of any who attacked them. This saved the day. The people of God were spared. And a potential holocaust became an annual holiday.

It is a wonderful story, but I believe it is more than that. Though my exploration continues and there is much more I expect to encounter, there is already more information than I can possibly share in the remaining pages of this book. But I will try to convey what has been shown to me.

Let's go back to how the fifth chapter of Esther begins:

> On the third day of the fast, Esther put on her royal robes and entered the
> inner court of the palace, just across from the king's hall. The king was sitting
> on his royal throne, facing the entrance. When he saw Queen Esther standing
> there in the inner court, he welcomed her and held out the gold scepter to her.
> So Esther approached and touched the end of the scepter.[5]

That first phrase, "on the third day," refers to the plan Esther detailed to her uncle: to fast for three days and nights before taking her life in her hands by going to the king uninvited. It is a simple indication that she stuck to the plan. But could it be more than that?

You may have already recognized in those words a phrase of recurring significance in the Bible. It was on the third day of creation that God commanded the waters to recede "and let dry ground appear."[6] The dry ground was revealed on the third day.

In the story of Abraham taking his son Isaac to Mount Moriah as a sacrifice, called "the binding of Isaac" by many, the text records, "On the third day of their journey, Abraham looked up and saw the place in the distance."[7] In other words, their destination was revealed on the third day.

In the story of Joseph, he had been sold into slavery by his brothers, only to have them later come before him when he was second-in-command of all Egypt and, not recognizing him, ask for grain to take home to the rest of their family. According to the Bible, it was "on the third day" that Joseph learned the inside story of his brothers' plot against him. When Moses led the Hebrews out of slavery in Egypt and they gathered at the base of Mount Sinai, God descended on the mountain and promised to meet them there. He told Moses, "Go to the people and consecrate them today and tomorrow, and let them wash their garments and be ready for the third day. For on the third day the LORD will come down on Mount Sinai in the sight of all the people."[8] On the third day, the Law was revealed to the people of God.

And so it goes, on and on in the Scriptures. The second chapter of John begins, "On the third day there was a wedding at Cana in Galilee."[9] That was the occasion of Jesus's first miracle, the turning of water into wine, which John explained by saying, "This, the first of his signs, Jesus did at Cana in Galilee, and manifested his glory."[10] In other words, "on the third day," Jesus's glory—His identity and power as the Son of God—was revealed.

And, of course, Jesus repeatedly referred to His coming resurrection in terms of the third day:

> From then on Jesus began to tell his disciples plainly that it was necessary for him to go to Jerusalem, and that he would suffer many terrible things at the hands of the elders, the leading priests, and the teachers of religious law. He would be killed, but on the third day he would be raised from the dead.[11]

On the third day Jesus was revealed as Lord of life and Conqueror of death, the Eternal One, the Elohim Alpha Omega.

I do not think it is coincidental that the Bible describes Esther arising and shining (see Isaiah 60:1) on the third day, no longer a hidden bride but revealed as one who would sacrifice her life for the deliverance of her people.

Such phrasing seems especially significant in light of the New Testament's repeated references to Jesus as bridegroom and the church, comprised of all those who have found new life through faith in Christ, as His bride. The culmination, of course, is the future marriage supper of the Lamb, described in the last book of the Bible as the final and irreversible union of Jesus with the church.

While I am aware of widely varying scholarly views of the last things, the promise of Jesus Christ's return has been a dominant theme in Christian thought and teaching for almost two thousand years. So it strikes me as of no little significance that embedded in the phrase "on the third day" (ביום השלישי) is a five-letter Hebrew word (שלהוב) that can be translated as "rapture."

Remember that one of the remarkable ways biblical Hebrew communicates meaning is in the precise letter structure of its words and phrases. Since Hebrew words are composed of common roots, it is important to understand the meaning of the two- and three-letter roots that are combined to form words. The consonant roots are composed of letters, each with their own hieroglyphic meaning, and as we have seen, words and names can be inserted into sections of the text at an equidistance in which there is an obvious connection. So it seems worthy to mention that embedded into the phrase "on the third day," from left to right at an EDLS of two, is the Hebrew word *shalhoub* ("rapture"), which begins with the three-letter root *shalah* (שלה) ("to draw out, to remove, to extract"):

Thus in Esther 5:1–2, in a scene in the drama that involves the bride being drawn out of her hiddenness (not only from her chamber but also out of the secrecy concerning her true identity as a Jew) and into the king's presence and favor—in an act that saved the lives and promoted the well-being of all her people—the structure of the Hebrew letters themselves suggests the possibility that Esther's story is my story and yours too: *a prophetic sign of the final act in the human drama.*

14

Do Not Hide the Truth

U pon my first discoveries in the Leningrad Codex, my natural inclination was to keep them hidden if for no other reason than to protect myself (and my family). Even though it seemed obvious that certain things were intended for me to find and that they seemed to answer so many of my life's questions and fulfill so many longings, I didn't fully understand them. I still don't. As with much of God's works and ways, just because I can recognize His hand doesn't mean I can read what He is writing.

There came a point in my research where I had independently verified all of the critical observations of my initial discovery. The translations were rock solid, the statistical significance was like nothing anyone had ever seen, and a large body of academic and scientific publications provided substantiation for my assertion that the Masoretic text of the Hebrew Bible possessed remarkable and virtually inexplicable characteristics. Any objection to the possibility that abundant intelligent information was encrypted into the text seemed to be based solely on ideological considerations—at least that's how I saw it. And though there was simply no escaping the fact that the key code and the encryptions connected with it possessed mysterious qualities, it was equally plain that I couldn't wield or manipulate the text like a magic wand or crystal ball.

The *Rocío Madonna* encryption was a perfect example. I had never heard of this tradition before I discovered that name encoded directly over the key code. As I stated earlier, I am not and never have been a Marian devotee. I was raised Catholic but had not been involved in the Catholic Church since my midteens. It was an empirical fact that the *Timotheus* key identified me and precise personal biographical information related to my immediate family, but it was also clear that the meaning and focus of the messages had no more to do with me than with anyone else.

It also seemed logical that the *Rocío Madonna* encryption was employed because millions of people in the modern world would not fail to recognize the connection between a well-known representation of the Virgin Mary and the perfect symmetrical intersection of detailed information that has always been associated with her. Interpreting the meaning of the phenomenon was another matter, but I was not going to turn my back on this marvel simply because it challenged my views and perspectives.

One night I was propped up in bed reading Haim Shore's *Coincidences in the Bible and in Biblical Hebrew* (which I mentioned in chapters 10 and 11). I was not only intrigued by Dr. Shore's research but also emotionally relieved by his observations and conclusions. This careful scientist wrote that he was perplexed by the results of his methodical experiments and stated bluntly in his preface that he was reluctant at first to publish his findings, knowing it would not likely burnish his career. Eventually, however, his academic integrity compelled him to publish, since he believed it would be dishonest to hide the results of his experiments.

If I were losing my mind, as I occasionally worried I might be, then at least I was losing it in good company.

THE SWORD AND THE STAFF

At the core of the oldest traditions of many cultures throughout the world is a basic concept that all understanding must stand on solid foundations. In Japanese culture it is called *kihon* ("the fundamental understanding of all things"). The term is usually used in reference to the basics that must be mastered first in the martial arts, but in a broader sense it refers to the essential lessons of life, the foremost being to act honorably and to stand in defense of the innocent. The same concept is embraced in the medieval notion of chivalry, with its emphasis on honor, valor, and generosity. The meaning and message of the crucified Jesus is the epitome of these principles.

Yet as powerful and universal as the message of the *Timotheus* and *Elohim Alef Tav* matrix is, I continued to discover still more in the text. Directly following *Timotheus* in the key matrix (Genesis 30) was more than just the word *key*. Interestingly, the code went on to spell the Japanese word *kihon*. And following that word is the Hebrew word *muwth* (meaning "to be put to death" or "to be executed"), which in turn is followed by the Hebrew word *dath* ("a royal edict or decree"), a word used only in the books of Esther and Daniel and always in the sense of a decree issued by the worldly power of gentile kings.

That unique embedded chain of the nine letters that spell *Timotheus,* combined with the ten Hebrew letters that follow the message, could be seen as producing a message that says,

Elohim, Alpha and Omega, honored of God, crucified and lifted up, put to death by official decree of the kings of the world.

That nineteen-letter encryption is followed by the Hebrew word meaning "manna," the bread that came down from heaven to feed the Israelites in the wilderness (see Exodus 16), which Jesus mentioned after the miraculous feeding of the five thousand:

I tell you the truth, anyone who believes has eternal life. Yes, I am the bread of life! Your ancestors ate manna in the wilderness, but they all died. Anyone who eats the bread from heaven, however, will never die. I am the living bread that came down from heaven. Anyone who eats this bread will live forever; and this bread, which I will offer so the world may live, is my flesh.[1]

Interestingly enough—though *interesting* seems like much too mild a word— turning back to the same tiny matrix, encoded in the text containing the key code and the word *manna,* at an equidistance of sixteen, are the following Hebrew letters: חבא אב ישוע.

It is a phrase that in English could be understood as "the hidden Father Jesus" or "the Father hidden in Jesus" (the phrase literally reads "hide Father Jesus"). Each of these codes form the matrix that appears in Figure 14.A.

Obviously, the shape on the left in Figure 14.A is a cruciform. But its extra length, aligning at the bottom with the second shape at the right, could also be seen as the outline of a sword. And, of course, the two symbols, appearing next to each other, might suggest the idea of a sword and a rod, both recurring biblical symbols of power and authority, particularly given the words and phrases from which they are formed.

Of course, the Scriptures compare the Word of God to a sword, double edged and razor sharp:

> For the word of God is alive and powerful. It is sharper than the sharpest
> two-edged sword, cutting between soul and spirit, between joint and marrow.
> It exposes our innermost thoughts and desires.[2]

The rod also occurs in Scripture and story as a symbol of power and protection. The familiar words of Psalm 23 mention the shepherd's rod: "Even when I walk through the darkest valley, I will not be afraid, for you are close beside me. Your rod and your staff protect and comfort me."[3] Psalm 2 refers to a rod in the hand of a king as symbolic of absolute power: "You will break them with an iron rod and smash them like clay pots."[4]

Most strikingly, however, the figures formed by the matrix found in Genesis 30 recall to me the passage in Revelation in which the triumphant, exalted Jesus is depicted in the most memorable symbolic terms:

> Then I saw heaven opened, and a white horse was standing there. Its rider was
> named Faithful and True, for he judges fairly and wages a righteous war. His
> eyes were like flames of fire, and on his head were many crowns. A name was
> written on him that no one understood except himself. He wore a robe
> dipped in blood, and his title was the Word of God. The armies of heaven,
> dressed in the finest of pure white linen, followed him on white horses. From
> his mouth came a sharp sword to strike down the nations. He will rule them

ק ב ו ת א מ ר ל א ה ז ב ד נ י א

ל ה י ס א ת י ז ב ד ט ו ב ה פ ע

ס י ז ב ל נ י א כ י ש י כ י ל ד

ת י ל ו ש ש ה ב נ י ם ו ת ק ר א

א ת ש מ ו ז ב ל ו ן ו א ח ר י ל

ד ה ב ת ו ת ק ר א א ת ש מ ה ד י

נ ה ו י ז כ ר א ל ה י ם א ת ר ח

ל ו י ש מ ע א ל י ה א ל ה י ם ו

י פ ת ח א ת ר ח מ ה ו ת ה ר ו ת

ל ד ב ן ו ת א מ ר א ס פ א ל ה י

ס א ת ח ר פ ת י ו ת ק ר א א ת ש

מ ו י ו ס ף ל א מ ר י ס ף י ה ו

ה ל י ב ן א ח ר ו י ה י כ א ש ר

י ל ד ה ה ר ח ל א ת י ו ס ף ו י א

מ ר י ע ק ב א ל ל ב ן ש ל ח נ י

ו א ל כ ה א ל מ ק ו מ י ו ל א ר

צ י ת נ ה א ת נ ש י ו א ת י ל ד

י א ש ר ע ב ד ת י א ת ך ב ה ן ו

א ל כ ה כ י א ת ה י ד ע ת א ת ע

ב ד ת י א ש ר ע ב ד ת י ך ו י א

מ ר א ל י ו ל ב ן א ס נ א מ צ א

ת י ח ן ב ע י נ י ד נ ח ש ת י ו

י ב ר כ נ י י ה ו ה ב ג ל ל ד ו

Figure 14.A. Vertical, top to bottom: *Timotheus, kihon, muwth, dath,* and *manna.* Horizontal, right to left: *Elohim Alef Tav.* Bottom right, top to bottom: literally "hide Father Jesus."

with an iron rod. He will release the fierce wrath of God, the Almighty, like juice flowing from a winepress. On his robe at his thigh was written this title: King of all kings and Lord of all lords.[5]

A sword and a rod. Those references to Elohim, Alpha and Omega, the Bread of Heaven, put to death by the decree of earthly kings, encoded in the matrix of Genesis 30 in the shape of a sword and a rod leave me scratching my head—and bowing it as well.

ELOHIM'S TRUTH

Slowly, over time, I have come to believe there were things I needed to do, things that were being asked of me. But what, exactly? I could discern hints and allusions, metaphors and parallels, miraculous signs and wonders, but still no straightforward "Go here" or "Do that."

Sometimes I felt like the boy Samuel in the Old Testament, who heard a distinct voice and call but needed Eli's help to know how to respond. At other times I have felt more like Saul of Tarsus in the New Testament, who was knocked for a loop and blinded at first and had to wait for the scales to drop from his eyes—yet still had years of training ahead of him.

I think God uses a variety of ways to get through to us or we would tend to rely on habit and technique rather than on Him.

As I was working on the last few chapters of this book I went back to the key-code matrix, back to where my discoveries in the text began, back to the place where I knew for certain that God was speaking to me, trying to get my attention. Once again I viewed the unequivocal testimony of *Yeshua Mashiach,* Jesus the Messiah, God Himself, the Creator of heaven and earth, who had come down to earth and entered the human experience through the womb of a young girl, only to be rejected and crucified by His fellow human beings. This was shown to me in such a miraculous way that it was as if I had witnessed His life and death and resurrection. But I wanted so badly for Him to speak to me clearly and tell me *what to do,* because I knew I lacked the courage and faith to do what someone less flawed than I, I'm certain, could do far better.

This time I stepped back, so to speak, by dialing the matrix open. I was still in the exact same section of Genesis where this all began for me. The entire key code was still in the expanded matrix but now back to an equidistance of sixteen, as I had originally found it.

I immediately saw the name of God—*Elohim*—appear as an unbroken vertical encryption in the middle of the matrix. I had never seen that before. It took me more than a few minutes to work out exactly what was written there. I could hardly believe my eyes. It was straightforward English syntax, easy for me to understand, undeniable. Thirteen straight Hebrew letters inside the key-code matrix spelled out "Do not hide Elohim's truth." (See Figure 14.B.)

As I have mentioned more than once, I have struggled for years to figure out what I should do with all these things. I have had hints and intimations, dreams and intuitions. I have invested years of prayer in trying to understand what it all might mean and what action I was supposed to take. I have come to believe I just needed to make an attempt to explain the matter the best I could, to the best of my understanding, to show why I believed it was so important—maybe even ultimately important. I have been repeatedly unsure of myself and of the best way to proceed, but this clear message of "Do not hide the truth" sealed the deal for me.

Anyone who has read the Bible knows that, more often than not, when a sign or message is given to an individual or to the people in general, warning or instruction soon follows. Matthew's gospel relates how the Magi, having been guided by a star to the newborn king, "returned to their own country by another route, for God had warned them in a dream not to return to Herod."[6] After telling Mary and Joseph that the infant Jesus had been "sent as a sign from God," Simeon told Mary, "A sword will pierce your very soul."[7] Similarly, the gospel writer says that after Joseph and Mary lived in exile in Egypt to escape King Herod's vicious pogrom, Joseph was given the all clear to return to Israel, but he was then warned in a subsequent dream to avoid Judea and settle instead in Nazareth.[8]

In any case, my part in the drama is ultimately a bit part. The lead belongs to the text itself, and it will not be upstaged. I am fully convinced that it will continue to speak long after I am gone. And, as will be seen in the remainder of this book, I, too, am guided and propelled forward by a sobering reality.

```
ל    א  ה  ו  י
ק    א  ל  ה
ה    ל  ו  ו
ר    צ  י  י
י    פ  י  י
א    נ  ו  ו
ס    א  ח  א
ק    ל  א  א
ר    ה  נ  ה
ו    י  ה
ת    מ  ב  ר
י    א  ש  ת
א    ת  ת  י
ל    צ  א
     ל  ו  א
```

Figure 14.B. Vertical, top to bottom: "Do not hide Elohim's truth."

Whatever comes of these discoveries—whether people ignore them or refute them, or whether these pages prompt others more astute and adept than I to explore the amazingly preserved text of the Hebrew Scriptures and to expand and improve upon my efforts—I choose to heed those words: "Do not hide the truth."

Whether the admonition against hiding Elohim's truth refers to the entirety of God's revelation from Genesis through Revelation or to the encoded messages that miraculously support that revelation or to the dire warning I will share in the next chapter, I knew I could no longer keep this information to myself.

Like Esther, it was time to step forward with the truth.

15

For Such a Time as This

Among the many questions I struggled with after discovering the chamberlain key and other codes in the Hebrew text, one nagged me mercilessly: Why now? After all, sages and scholars had combed the ancient text of the Hebrew Scriptures for generations. Many great minds had suspected or hinted at the secret and sacred treasures hidden in the uniquely preserved grid of the text. And, of course, more recently, others *have* examined and documented startling indications of coded information in the Hebrew Bible. Why would the key code and such messages as "Do not hide Elohim's truth" have been waiting for me to discover them when I did?

I believe at least part of the answer is that a warning lies in the codes that awaited my lifetime—and yours—an urgent caution that applies specifically and ominously to the twenty-first century. These encryptions in the Hebrew Bible are so disturbing and alarming that I hesitate even now to disclose them. I have alluded to them before in general terms as they relate to themes in the book of Esther and the history of Israel.

But these messages are not only historical in nature: They are modern. They are present. They are here and now. They are soon and very soon.

THE BROKEN CROSS

In 1956 John F. Kennedy and his wife, Jacqueline, purchased a home in a small neighborhood of Langley, Virginia. The lovely estate, called Hickory Hill, was later sold to the president's brother Robert F. Kennedy and his wife, Ethel.

I was born four years later in that same neighborhood, in 1960, the year John Kennedy was elected president of the United States. Like all the Catholic families in that little community, we attended Saint Luke's Church, a parish church not a mile down the road on Georgetown Pike. I was too young, of course, to understand the tragic events that would soon rock our community.

On November 22, 1963, President Kennedy was assassinated in Dallas, Texas. His murder horrified not only the American people but the entire free world. When his brother Senator Robert Kennedy was assassinated on June 5, 1968, I was old enough to witness the impact on the lives of his children, with whom I had attended church and school. My older brothers were even more intimately acquainted with the family, and those days powerfully affected them for the rest of their lives.

We all grew up with a shadowy sense that there were forces in this world that none of us understood. And no matter how privileged or protected people may feel themselves to be, they could still fall victim to those forces.

Much of my research and scrutiny of the encryptions in the Hebrew text has involved a constant process of tracing and retracing my steps. I would make a discovery that would then make sense of something I'd seen previously, like assembling a jigsaw puzzle. As more connections were made and the picture began to come to life, puzzle pieces that had been set aside found their place. As I realized how much coded information clustered around the key-code location in Genesis 30, I began to scrutinize any possible two-dimensional array, which is how I found the code I will now describe.

The matrix in Figure 15.A appears in the center of Genesis 30, where the key code and the reference to the crucified Messiah are located. In fact, the entire key code passes through this matrix horizontally at an equidistance of sixteen, but showing this here would require a page too wide. However, the vertical encryption, bottom to top, clearly reads "inaugurated President Kennedy dead."

ר א ל א מ ר א ש ת י פ ן י ה ר
א ש ה מ ב ו נ ת ו ח ת כ א ל ה מ
ת ק ר א א ת ש מ ו ז ב ל ו ן ו
י א מ ר ל ב ז ל י ע ק ב ה נ ה
ו ת ה ה ד ב ר כ י ח פ ץ ב ב ת י
א ל ב ת מ ט ר ד ב ת מ י ז ה ב
ס פ ח ן ב ע י נ י ו ו י ש ר ת
ץ מ צ ר י ס ו ק מ ו ש ב ע ש נ
י ה י ש ל כ ם א ח ו נ ג ד ל ו
ל ה י מ ס ו י ש י מ נ י ל א ב ל
א ד נ י ל א נ ש א ר ל פ נ י א
א מ צ א א ת ח ז ב ע י ן כ ם
י צ ח ק ו א ל ה י י ע ק ב ו י
ל כ ו ע ב ד ו ו ת ב ן ל א י ן
ל מ ע ן ת ד ע כ י א ז ן כ י ה
ש ה ב נ ע ר י נ ו ו ב ז ק נ י
ל מ ה ר ל ש ל ח ם ן ה א ר ץ
ע י ה ו ה ב י ו ס ה ה ו א א ת

Figure 15.A. Vertically, bottom to top: "Inaugurated President Kennedy dead."
Diagonal arm of the figure on the left: "America" or "American." Diagonal
arm of the figure on the right: "Leprous infection/scab appears/rises up."

The Hebrew word *nasiy'* (נשיא) is a four-letter word used 131 times in the Tanakh, the Hebrew Bible. It is typically translated as "prince," meaning a ruler or highest official. This encryption uses an even more specific form indicating "the president." The diagonal broken crossbeam on the left is a seven-letter word that translates to "American." Figure 15.B shows the actual Google Translate screen shot listing the straightforward translation of the Hebrew characters into modern English.

Figure 15.B. The broken cross symbol in the Hebrew text with the Google Translate dialog box indicating the English translation of the center line of the text and the diagonal text at left.

The broken crossbeam on the right combines the two Hebrew words *s'eth* (שאת), used several times in the text and translated as "uprising or swelling infection," and *quwm* (קומ), which means "to rise up" or "come on to the scene"—often with a hostile implication. So the diagonal portions of the figure can be interpreted as communicating the idea of "a leprous infection rising up or coming on to the scene in America." Combined with the vertical part of the symbol, we connect the phrase "inaugurated President Kennedy dead" with a terrible infection or cancer rising up and coming on to the scene in America.

What can this possibly mean?

The image formed by these phrases is unmistakable. The message is conveyed in the symbol of the broken cross: the Toten Rune used in Hitler's Third Reich as the rune of death.

Figure 15.C. The Toten Rune (or "death rune") displayed at the funeral of a Norwegian National Socialist. The symbol to the left of the Toten Rune is the *sieg rune* of an SS member. The sun cross on the right is the emblem of the Norwegian Nazi party.

The Nazi *Schutzstaffel,* or *SS-Runen* (illustrated in Figure 15.C.), used the symbol on flags and uniforms as well as German death notices and gravestones (rather than a Christian cross, as had previously been the custom). Also, as a perversion of the cross (upside down and broken), it has often been used in Satanic cults and rituals.

What is really being communicated in this strange combination of words and symbols? What possible connection could there be between a reference to an assassinated American president, a rising infection of some kind, and the Nazi death rune it forms?

A Mirror Institution

I have struggled over the answer to that question for a long time and expect to continue to puzzle over it for some time to come. But this I know: the intelligence behind the encryptions I've found in the text seems to use words, phrases, and names that are easily recognizable but not always easily understood or applied. The messages are placed in the text as a sort of sound amplifier or loudspeaker to draw our attention. And they also seem to work with their locations in the text to turn up the volume a few more notches.

In this case the death rune crosses the passage in Genesis 30 where I first discovered the key code. It is also the passage relating the births of the children of Leah and Rachel, the children of Israel (the name *Israel* is given just two chapters later, in Genesis 32). It would not be surprising, therefore, if the references to an assassination, a growing cancer, and a Nazi symbol somehow related to the children of Israel.

Some historians believe that various high-ranking members of the Nazi Party escaped capture at the end of World War II and, partnering with family members and others around the world, were able to utilize the vast wealth the Third Reich had amassed to establish a complex web of international investments and business enterprises. Some suggest the mastermind of this post-WWII scheme was none other than the former Nazi Party chancellor Martin Bormann, one of the few men in the Third Reich who answered only to Hitler himself.[1] Such vast wealth in the hands of those connected to perpetrators of the Holocaust, the so-called Final Solution that nearly fulfilled Haman's murderous plot against the children of Israel, could still promote the darkest objectives of Hitler's regime. Such a combination of wealth, ruthlessness, and secrecy could conceivably attain worldwide influence—so long as its true nature was never made known.

Sound crazy? Fantastical? Just another conspiracy theory? Perhaps. But consider the following.

Around the same time that I discovered the Nazi death-rune code in Genesis 30, I became curious if the nefarious organization of the Nazi regime was indeed being used as a clearly understood metaphor representing the type of secret murder and terror employed to overthrow the free will of our nation or, for that matter, any free nation. I simply combined the Hebrew word for "organization" with the standard Hebrew spelling of *Nazi* and checked to see if this eight-letter phrase was encrypted anywhere in the text.

Shockingly, the phrase did indeed appear as an equidistant encryption. But it turned out to be far more extensive than my eight-letter query. It was actually only a portion of a more extensive thirteen-letter code appearing in the Hebrew text of Psalms, the collection of ancient songs of God's people. I believe it not only sheds light on the death-rune encryption but also contributes to an urgent and important message for our times. (See Figure 15.D.)

The message is stunningly straightforward. From bottom to top, the first four letters spell the Hebrew word *muwcad* (מוסד). This is almost always read as "foundation," meaning the original structure upon which something is built. In modern Hebrew it is usually translated as "institution."

The word that follows is the Hebrew spelling commonly used for and is quite clearly "Nazi." The last five letters comprise the modern Hebrew phrase "a mirror." (See Figure 15.D.)

These letters translate so easily and plainly into English in Google Translate, as Figure 15.E shows on page 162, that there can be no doubt as to their meaning: "a mirror Nazi institution." What a loaded phrase! An institution that is a mirror image of the Nazi regime, something that reflects the same values and goals, would be terrifying, to be sure. But there is more in that matrix.

As you can see in Figures 15.D and E, the vertical line of the text in the matrix is crossed by a line of letters exactly in the middle.

The Hebrew letters that form the horizontal line of the cruciform shape coincide with the date of the twenty-third day of the month Elul in the Hebrew calendar. In the year 2001 in the Gregorian calendar, which we use in the Western world, that date is September 11, the day the United States was struck by a well-coordinated

ט י ה ה ט ו ל ו א פ ת ע י ק ו

י ה ו ה ה צ ב א ו ת ש י מ ו

י ר נ י כ א י ש א ש ר י ע

כ י ע ת ה ה ר א י ת י ב ע י

א י ס ע ל י ר ו ש ל ס ו ע

י ע נ י א ל ה י כ י ה כ י

י ך ג ו ר ל י ח ב ל י ס נ

ל ד ב ג י א צ ל מ ו ת ל א

ו י ה י ה ו א צ ו ה ו י ע

ש כ י ג ר א נ כ י ע מ ד ת

י ו ן פ י י ד ב ר ח כ מ ו

ב ל ו ל ת מ ס י ה ל ד נ פ

נ ו א ל מ ו ש ע ו ת ו ל

מ א ו ר ו ש מ ש א ת ה ה צ

ה ע ד י ס ו א ל נ ה ר י ו

Figure 15.D. Vertically, bottom to top: "institution," "Nazi," and "a mirror." The horizontal letters correspond to a date that translates to September 11.

ט י ט ה ה ל ו א פ ת ע י ק ו
י ה ו ה צ ב ב א ו ת ש י מ ו
י ר נ י כ א י ש א ש ר י ע
כ י ע ת ה ה ר א י ת י ב ע י
א י ס ע ל י י ר ו ש ל ם ו ע
י ע נ י א ל ה י כ י ה כ י
י ד ג ו ר ל י י ח ב ל י ם נ
ל י ד ב ג י א צ ל מ ו ת ל א
ו י ה י ה ו א צ ו ה ו י ע
ש כ י ג ר א נ כ י ע מ ד ת
י ו ן פ י י ד ב ר ח כ מ ו
ב ל ו ל ת מ ס י ה ל ד ן פ
נ ו א ל ל מ ו ש ע ו ת ו ל
מ א ו ר ו ש מ ש א ת ה ה צ
ה ע ד י ם ו א ל נ ה ר י ו

Figure 15.E. Google Translate box depicting the translation of the vertical phrase, also shown in Figure 15.D.

series of attacks aimed at targets in New York and Washington, DC, that took the lives of nearly three thousand innocent people.

These striking encryptions appear at an equidistance of two in the precise center of this extremely familiar verse in Psalms:

> Yea, though I walk through the valley of the shadow of death,
> I will fear no evil;
> For You are with me;
> Your rod and Your staff, they comfort me.[2]

On the evening of September 11, 2001, at the end of a day in which thousands had perished in the terrorist attacks, President George W. Bush addressed the shaken people of the United States on television. In his remarks, which lasted fewer than five minutes, he asked for prayer and quoted one familiar verse of Scripture from Psalm 23, in which the "mirror Nazi institution" code is found.

A coincidence? Probably. But a striking one nevertheless.

THE SPIRIT OF HAMAN AND HITLER

My experience with the encryptions in the Hebrew Bible leads me to believe that these messages I've just revealed are correlated not only with each other but also with the remarkable messages swirling around the book of Esther and the story of the fifth-century BC holocaust attempted by Haman. In fact, I see a confluence of encryptions and current events that make the hairs on the back of my neck stand up.

Before World War II there were an estimated seventeen million Jews in the world. After the Holocaust perpetrated by Nazi Germany and its European allies and collaborators, only eleven million remained. Today, even with six million Jews living in Israel, the worldwide Jewish population is much smaller—roughly fourteen million—than it was at the beginning of the Nazi atrocities.

The defeat of Nazi Germany did not eradicate the spirit of Haman and Hitler. Far from it. The twenty-first century has already witnessed the rise of a violent strain of that spirit, not only among brutal terrorist organizations such as Hamas, Hezbollah, al Qaeda, and ISIS, but also in virulently anti-Semitic states such as Iran (located where the spirit of Haman originated, in ancient Persia), where leaders repeatedly vow the annihilation of Israel. It is a contagion so widespread that author and columnist Charles Krauthammer calls the Middle East "today the heart of global anti-Semitism, a veritable factory of anti-Jewish literature, films, blood libels and calls for violence, indeed for another genocide."[3]

Nor is the spirit of Haman and Hitler confined to the Middle East. Recent years have seen a resurgence of hatred and violence toward Jews in Europe. For every atrocity that makes headlines, such as the 2015 terrorist attacks in Paris that left 130 people dead and hundreds wounded, many more have become so commonplace they hardly merit a mention in the evening news, such as the murder of a rabbi and three children at a Jewish school in the French city of Toulouse or the terror attack that killed four at the Jewish Museum in Brussels, Belgium. In fact, says Dr. Moshe Kantor, president of the European Jewish Congress, "Many streets in our European cities have become hunting grounds for Jews, and some Jews are now forced to avoid community institutions and synagogues as a result. . . . Some are choosing to leave the continent, many are afraid to walk the streets, and even more are retreating behind high walls and barbed wire. This has become the new reality of Jewish life in Europe."[4]

As the death rune seems to portend, that cancer is spreading and growing in the United States as well. The Anti-Defamation League recently reported a 21 percent increase in the total number of anti-Semitic incidents in the United States,[5] including a deadly shooting at two Jewish facilities in Kansas as well as dozens of assaults and hundreds of acts of terrorism and vandalism targeting synagogues and Jewish-owned businesses and community centers. And a recent study from the Louis D. Brandeis Center for Human Rights Under Law and Connecticut's Trinity College reported that anti-Semitism is on the rise on college campuses in the United States.[6] Add these horrible atrocities to the murder and public executions of Christians and Jews around the world by radical Islamic terrorist organizations, and we begin to see more clearly what might be meant by "a mirror Nazi institution," one in which murder and genocide are justified to achieve a dark ideological objective.

I believe the Bible encryptions contain a warning and a challenge that parallel the biblical account of Esther. History and Scripture, as well as modern research and current events, bear witness to the tragic reality that Haman's work continues in today's world. Although Haman was hanged and the Nazis defeated, the spirit that animated them lives and may be far more widespread, well connected, and well financed than any of us can imagine. I believe the chamberlain key code and its mind-boggling time lock—along with the resulting messages I've found about the reliability of the Bible, the identity and saving work of the Messiah, the command not to hide Elohim's truth, and the warning of a spreading, deadly cancer of anti-Semitic hatred and violence in our modern world—have been revealed "for such a time as this."[7]

Those who follow Jesus in the twenty-first century must lead the way in opposing the spirit of Haman and Hitler and the spread of anti-Semitism. Of all people, Christians, who "are all children of God through faith in Christ Jesus,"[8] must stand against bigotry and racism in all forms, no matter how acceptable or even popular it may become and no matter how powerful and intimidating its proponents may be. As Professor David A. Rausch wrote,

> It is amazing how the remembrance of the Holocaust and the Nazi Era is intrinsically linked to our global future. . . .
>
> It is with great joy that we acknowledge the thousands of Christians who have . . . faced the cancer of religious and racial prejudice squarely. Just as those few Christians who loved their Jewish neighbors and their Jewish Jesus enough to stand firm against evil and help during the Holocaust, these modern resisters fight the monster of racial and religious bigotry wherever it raises its ugly head. They teach their young people and work with their peers to provide a legacy of love and light. In the words of sociologist Nechama Tec, herself a Jewish survivor of the Holocaust, these modern followers of Jesus are like their earlier counterparts—"lights piercing the darkness."[9]

We must not be tricked or seduced or pressured into participating in, consenting to, or even turning a blind eye to the spirit of Haman and Hitler. We must act as a twenty-first-century Esther. We must "shine like stars in the dark world."[10] We must rise and take hold of the King's authority and publish the timeless message of faith and courage in a time of great peril.

If we perish, we perish only to the things of this world.

If we are preserved to battle on, then let it be, in all humility, with the sword of truth and the rod of righteousness.

We never have to wonder *how* we must do this. We have the example of Jesus Christ, our Creator, the Alef and Tav, the Alpha and Omega, the Beginning and the End.

Actionable Intelligence

W hile I know that much remains to be explored and discovered, I am utterly convinced that the chamberlain key and the discoveries it opened up are profoundly important. If nothing else, the encryptions in the codex point to the absolute truth of the apostle Peter's words:

> We have even greater confidence in the message proclaimed by the prophets.
> You must pay close attention to what they wrote, for their words are like a
> lamp shining in a dark place—until the Day dawns, and Christ the Morning
> Star shines in your hearts.[1]

I can never again doubt the messages proclaimed in the Bible, because I have seen the amazing complexity and intricacy of the encoded text. And the various discoveries imparted through the surprising appearance of the *Rocío Madonna* encryption encourage me to believe that still more mysteries await and more truths lie hidden, perhaps from a yet-to-be-discovered text more ancient than the Leningrad Codex.

In addition, the beautifully encrypted information in the Hebrew text clearly reinforces to me that Jesus is the Messiah—the Elohim Alef Tav of Genesis 1:1, the Alpha and Omega of Revelation 21:6, the Timothy Vav Vav who was crucified with nails in each of His hands, the Bright Morning Star, the Word of God, the Son of David, He who is honored of God, the Crucified One, the Risen Lord, and the King of kings. His coming is prophesied in the Law and the Prophets, and His identity is woven in even the tiniest strokes and spaces of the Hebrew text.

With my renewed belief in the Scriptures and the Savior has come a growing awareness of the dangers arrayed against Jews and Christians—and the need for all of us to be vigilant against the forces of darkness that animate (and often unite) twenty-first-century anti-Semitism and global terrorism.

Finally, as I have pondered these mysteries, I have recently encountered a few correlations I had not seen earlier. In Revelation, the last book of the Bible, Jesus referred to Himself as "the bright morning star,"[2] using a term that first-century readers would have recognized as a direct reference to what we know as the planet Venus when it shines brightly in the east just before the dawning of a new day. This seems to be a loaded reference, not only because the Magi saw a star in the east and followed it to find the infant Jesus in Bethlehem, but also because of the words Jesus Himself used in referring to His Second Coming:

For as the lightning flashes *in the east* and shines to the west, so it will be when the Son of Man comes. . . .

And they will see the Son of Man coming on the clouds of heaven with power and great glory. And he will send out his angels with the mighty blast of a trumpet, and they will gather his chosen ones from all over the world—from the farthest ends of the earth and heaven.[3]

Before that day dawns, Scripture says something will happen first, an event foretold in the Hebrew Scriptures:

For behold, the day is coming, burning like an oven, when all the arrogant and all evildoers will be stubble. The day that is coming shall set them ablaze, says the LORD of hosts, so that it will leave them neither root nor branch. But for you who fear my name, the sun of righteousness shall rise with healing in its wings. You shall go out leaping like calves from the stall. And you shall tread down the wicked, for they will be ashes under the soles of your feet, on the day when I act, says the LORD of hosts.

Remember the law of my servant Moses, the statutes and rules that I commanded him at Horeb for all Israel.

Behold, I will send you Elijah the prophet before the great and awesome day of the LORD comes. And he will turn the hearts of fathers to their children and the hearts of children to their fathers, lest I come and strike the land with a decree of utter destruction.[4]

Although the exact nature of the event foretold in this prophecy is not revealed, it is clear its purpose is to avert some grave consequence. And the allusions to all the burning and blazing and ashes in this prophecy seem especially cogent in light of one of the most stunning encryptions I found in the Hebrew text. By combining the hidden name for the Messiah ("honored of God") with the Hebrew word for *star*, I discovered a ten-letter compound "Timothy star" that had a perfectly appropriate contextual meaning and a many-millions-to-one probability of appearing by chance in the text at any equidistance.

This encryption begins in 1 Kings 17:13, where the name of the prophet Elijah, in its standard five-letter spelling in biblical Hebrew, crossed through the encryption, giving the code the unmistakable form of a sword along with, on the left side of the matrix, the eight-letter phrase "rain of star fire" at an equidistance of two.

In Jesus's first advent, He linked John the Baptist with "Elijah, the one the prophets said would come."[5] Some expect a similar scenario before the Second Coming of Jesus, when a figure like Elijah will appear to herald that day.

In Jewish tradition, Elijah is expected to return just before the coming of the Messiah and resolve all controversy regarding the Torah and the prophetical writings so God's people will be prepared to receive the true Messiah. Elijah's role is to alleviate confusion and return the children to the true faith and understanding of their ancient fathers.

It may be that now is indeed the very moment these prophecies are being fulfilled.

תישׁשכרויכההובעעשׁאבגבחתוןאשרלפלשׁתיﬦﬡונדבוכלישׁראלצ
גהקﬦﬢנהברﬡשׁנהוהוﬡצﬡﬣﬡﬨליוׁלﬢנﬢﬨﬠשׂיבﬡﬣﬧנהﬥיﬦﬣﬡﬦ
סﬡﬥ﬩ﬣﬥﬢ﬩ﬡﬥﬡﬢﬤ﬩הּ﬩הּ﬩ﬠ﬩﬩הּﬦﬨﬦהּ﬩
נﬥﬦﬢﬡﬦﬨﬦﬢﬦדּ﬩דּﬧﬡﬦﬡ﬩ﬥﬡﬥﬨדּﬤﬦ﬩ﬡ﬩ﬨﬢﬤﬢﬧדּﬣ﬩הּﬠהּﬥהּﬤ﬩ﬦﬥﬠ
גﬢﬦדּﬦﬧﬦדּגּדּדּﬠﬥﬦﬢדּﬧﬥﬤדּﬦ﬩ﬦﬥﬡﬨﬥﬣﬤﬡגּﬦ﬩ﬣﬥﬦﬢﬣﬤﬧ﬩
בﬤﬡﬨדּﬢדּﬥﬦ﬩דּדּדּדּ﬩דּ﬩דּﬠﬠדּﬡ﬩דּﬦﬡﬦﬣ﬩דּﬥﬧﬡﬥﬦﬥﬤﬥﬡדּﬧﬦדּﬠ
ﬠﬢﬠ﬩﬩﬩﬩דּﬦﬧﬦﬧﬦﬥﬦﬤﬡﬢהּﬦﬦהּﬦﬡﬦﬥ﬩דּדּﬧﬧﬡדּ﬩ﬧדּﬢדּﬦﬢﬢﬨﬦﬢדּﬠﬥﬦﬡדּﬧדּדּ
תﬢ﬩ﬥﬤﬦﬦ﬩ﬦﬦדּﬠﬦדּדּ﬩דּﬢ﬩ﬤדּﬤﬦﬥﬤﬤﬦﬥﬤ﬩דּﬤﬥﬦ﬩דּ﬩ﬡדּדּדּﬥהּﬥהּדּהּﬨהּﬢﬧדּﬦדּﬦﬥדּ﬩
ק﬩ﬣﬦﬦדּﬥﬦﬣﬡﬧﬦﬦדּﬦדּﬣﬦﬥﬦﬨﬢ﬩﬩דּﬧﬡﬥדּ﬩ﬥﬠﬦﬠדּﬡﬥﬢﬤדּדּﬥﬡהּﬡﬦﬧﬥﬦﬦ
ה﬩ﬦﬤﬢﬥﬨﬦﬦדּﬧﬢדּדּדּﬧﬦﬦדּ﬩ﬥﬦ﬩ﬥדּﬨﬦﬥﬤדּדּﬦﬨדּדּהּ﬩דּדּדּﬦﬥהּדּדּדּﬦﬡﬦﬦ﬩דּדּﬦ﬩
ﬤﬧﬦﬢדּדּﬦﬦﬥﬦﬧﬧﬦהּדּ﬩דּﬦﬧﬦדּﬦדּﬦﬥﬤדּדּדּﬦﬦﬥﬦﬥדּדּﬦﬦדּﬧﬦﬦדּדּ﬩דּדּﬦﬦדּדּﬦﬥדּﬦדּדּ
ה﬩דּﬦדּ﬩דּﬦﬤדּ﬩ﬦﬦדּﬦﬥדּﬦﬨדּﬦדּ﬩דּﬦדּ﬩ﬦ﬩דּﬥﬦﬨדּﬦﬥדּדּדּﬥהּדּהּﬥדּהּדּדּהּדּﬦהּדּהּﬦדּהּדּהּדּהּדּ

Figure 16.A. Vertically, top to bottom: "Timothy star." Horizontal at right (forming the cross-guard of the sword), right to left: "Elijah." Horizontal at left, left to right: "rain of star fire."

The fact that my birth date (the twenty-third of Sh'vat, 5720, or the twenty-first of February 1960) is the only full date (day/month/year) I can find encrypted in the Hebrew Bible (and intersected with a phrase that mirrors my grandfather's cryptic name) does more than tie together in the text the many strange correspondences related to my ancestry. The key code's very precise time lock looks to be part of a series of signals indicating a critical period in human events: the final act of the human drama, the resolution of conflicts, the gathering from the scattering, the messianic triumph that brings order out of the chaos, the beginning of the end times. Could the discovery of the chamberlain key—the key code, the messages pointing to the Messiah, and the warnings of a mirror Nazi institution inciting terror and tragedy—be harbingers of what the Hebrew Scriptures often call "the Day of the Lord"?

I am hardly alone in seeing dreadful portents in the horrific acts of cruelty and terror perpetrated in the world today. And I am increasingly persuaded that we do not have the leisure to ponder these things for too long.

If the time lock of my birth date, February 21, 1960, is indeed some kind of cue, the time remaining may be short.

My long journey of adventure and discovery began with a star hidden in the darkness, stored away in the attic of my childhood home. It was as real and solid as this world itself and was put there by my father.

In time, led by the star, so to speak, I explored every box and crate and crevice of that attic. It would require no stretch of imagination to say I have been led by that star to this day and to this place where I find myself, perhaps something like the Magi, gazing on wonders far beyond my ken (and my pay grade).

Now, as then, I have discovered things that delight and mystify me, things I believe have somehow been placed there by the Father's hand, things that only increase my desire to explore and learn. My hope in writing this book is not to provoke unwarranted fear or, certainly, to imply I have all the answers but instead to invite investigation and consideration—to encourage others to take a closer look not only at the ancient Hebrew Scriptures and the remarkable Hebrew language but also at New Testament writings that appear to be interwoven with the Hebrew text in ways barely imagined before now.

I hope these pages will do for you what this journey of discovery has done for me: deepen and broaden your appreciation of the Bible as the Word of God. The Bible is a multilayered, multifaceted, multitextured revelation of God and His ways. It is "inspired by God and is useful to teach us what is true and to make us realize what is wrong in our lives."[6] It is "alive and powerful . . . sharper than the sharpest two-edged sword, cutting between soul and spirit, between joint and marrow."[7] It is inexpressibly and unfathomably complex and mysterious. It can change your life in an instant but will take many lifetimes to explore.

I also hope *The Chamberlain Key* and the various doors it has opened reinforce in you, as they have in me, an immeasurably stronger conviction about and devotion to Jesus, whose identity and mission are central to the codes contained in the text. I know as I have never known before that He is Elohim. He is Alef and Tav, Alpha and Omega, First and Last. He is the One who is honored of God, "the image of the invisible God, the firstborn over all creation . . . the beginning and the firstborn from among the dead, so that in everything he might have the supremacy."[8]

Some will object to my observations, suggesting that I am going outside of the Scriptures to promote an agenda of some kind. But I hope it is clear enough by now that I have sought with all my energy and insight to not exceed the boundaries of the Word of God but only to venture more deeply within them. The Word is a "sure word of prophecy,"[9] and the deeper one explores it, the more apparent that truth becomes.

Like this vast universe and the ecosystems of this planet God has created, there is far more to the Word of God than our limited minds can conceive: structures within structures, layers atop layers, systems intertwined with systems, all supporting one another and working together as one unified and interconnected whole in which is "hidden every wonder and every mystery, and in her treasures is sealed every beauty of wisdom."[10]

Things to Come

One dreary winter morning as I sat at my desk doing paperwork, my phone rang. Not only was I surprised at who was calling, I was once again put in the position of both trying to explain my preposterous story in a nutshell to an eminent academic and appealing to him for assistance.

Dr. Eugene Ulrich is a professor of Hebrew scripture and theology at the University of Notre Dame, a chief editor of the biblical texts included in the Dead Sea Scrolls, one of three general editors of the Scrolls International Publication Project, and a fellow of the American Academy of Arts and Sciences. It amazed me that he would contact me, an antiquities dealer and appraiser, which I imagine translates in his mind into a less heroic version of Indiana Jones. But his brother, a valued client of long standing, had persuaded him to call. So I gave him a synopsis of what I'd been doing and waited for him to hang up the phone. He didn't.

I went on to tell him that I have long been on the lookout for something I'd often been told does not exist, something every archivist, museum curator, and black-market antiquities dealer believes has been long lost: a complete Torah scroll that predates the Christian era, though I would be content with even a scroll fragment that contained the key code, these four verses from the book of Genesis, a scrap of bleached animal hide no bigger than a business card.

Dr. Ulrich confirmed that as far as he was aware, the Leningrad Codex was indeed the oldest extant Hebrew text of Genesis 30:20–23. However, after some double-checking, he did offer an intriguing observation. He told me that based on his examination of the Greek Septuagint, we could be certain that the letter sequence in that portion of the Leningrad Codex was the same as the Hebrew text from which the Septuagint was translated in the third century BC. In other words, the key code was undoubtedly pre-Christian. Nothing I was able to uncover had ever contradicted this, but hearing a biblical Hebrew scholar of his caliber confirm it certainly made my day.

Within a few weeks I had formalized an arrangement with Dr. Ulrich. He would assist me in matters relating to the translation of biblical Hebrew as well as ancient Greek and Latin. This would provide me with the ability to not only double-check my translations of encrypted information in the text but also pick his brain on delicate and perplexing issues regarding the current state of research concerning ancient biblical texts.

I never expected him to endorse my conclusions, but it was a great relief to have him looking over my shoulder. And his expert assessment enabled me to check off (for the time being, at least) one item on the daunting list I was compiling of the next steps to take.

New Technologies to Explore

Almost from the beginning of my exploration of early biblical texts, I have wondered if encrypted information in it might point to a specific location (or locations) where ancient Hebrew scribes or rabbis had placed important artifacts for safekeeping. Given what we know of the Masoretes and their strict protocols, as well as the reverence of Jewish thinkers and leaders for their sacred texts over many centuries, it seems highly probable they would have made a supreme effort to protect these writings (as, in fact, we know they did in many well-documented cases).

It also seems likely that such measures would have been both farsighted and ingenious. They knew the prophets had foretold that the children of Israel would be scattered throughout the nations of the world, but they also knew that God had promised they would return to their homeland. Could it be that their greatest treasure—the words of God—might not only have been protected but also encoded, perhaps by divine inspiration, against a time when all these things and events would come together?

Energized by the fact that some of the most statistically significant encrypted information seems to deal with matters related to the king's treasure house and royal archives, I have felt a sense of urgency to apply what I've learned about the codex, along with information from those who might subsequently offer correction or assistance, to locate any ancient manuscripts or artifacts that could shed further light on the most important body of writings the world has ever known: the Bible.

What treasures await discovery, perhaps before our very eyes?

Things are moving rapidly in that direction. The funding I needed to pursue further research has been approved. A customized computer program will allow me much greater capacity to explore and analyze the biblical texts (or any manuscript, for that matter) and accelerate my research tenfold.

A website (www.chamberlainkey.com) will soon be launched that will allow any interested person, scholar and nonscholar alike, to ask questions, offer insights, express opinions, and become part of the ongoing research and exploration. The website will offer updates as well as pool knowledge, intuition, and inspiration from interested people representing diverse fields and backgrounds around the world, a synergy I look forward to with great excitement.

In the meantime, with skilled support, I will revisit the most remarkable anomalies in the codex to see what has been overlooked.

New Roads to Travel

According to the father of information theory, Claude Shannon, "The more improbable an event the more information it conveys."[1] In the spring of 2016, I found myself sitting in a spacious conference room trying to summarize for a group of editors, marketers, and publicists what I planned to lay out for the public when my book was released the following year. The manuscript was written, but there were still many decisions to make. I'd prepared a presentation to capture the current status of a remarkable story that was still rapidly unfolding.

Over the next hour I clicked one slide after another, from the first stunning key-code encryption in the Leningrad Codex to recently discovered coded information that was perhaps too sensitive to publish (at least for now) but important for those in the room to know. There was also personal biographical documentation so important in extending our initial key code in Genesis 30.

A fortunate turn of events gave me the extra time I needed to gather and digest new information from southern Spain. This first improbable event had produced so much actionable intelligence that my only dilemma was deciding which location I should fly off to next and which collection or archive to explore. I felt like a kid in a candy factory!

THE ROCÍO MADONNA AND THE TEMPLE OF SOLOMON

Perhaps the most exciting immediate development in our continuing research revolves around the Virgin of El Rocío and its connections with early Christian Jews and the Spanish monarchy. Shortly after returning from Spain in 2015, my son Abe and I were able to extend our identification of the sixteen hidden symbols on the El Rocío statue not just to the larger tradition of Marian devotion but also to a compacted section of the Hebrew Bible.

To appreciate this connection for yourself, I encourage you to read 2 Chronicles 2:3 through the end of the fifth chapter. This is where you will find the building specifications for the first temple: the temple of Solomon. As you read, make a note each time you encounter a word or phrase that describes one of the sixteen symbols hidden on the clothing of the Rocío Madonna. You will find the ark and the cup and many of the other hidden symbols referred to specifically. But the code that opens up the full extent of this phenomenon is encrypted at an equidistance of 635 precisely over this section of text. It is הארון מפתח, the *arown maphteach* ("the ark key" or "the key to the ark"). And in this case *maphteach* is the precise word spelling translated as "key" in Isaiah 22:22:

And the key of the house of David will I lay upon his shoulder; so he shall open, and none shall shut; and he shall shut, and none shall open. (KJV)

This remarkable correlation of thematic and encrypted elements further supports our suspicion that the Rocío Madonna tradition may indeed represent much more than a symbolic allusion to the Virgin Mary as the ark of the covenant—the vessel of the Word of God. Rather, the entire tradition, as sponsored by the likes of King Alfonso X, may actually be the overt reflection of a very covert reality. If we have intuited correctly, then the message of the sixteen hidden symbols seems rather simple and direct. These symbols are the arown maphteach, the key to the ark, the sacred place where the Word of God is housed and protected.

As we've come to understand, the search for older biblical texts, and especially a pre-Christian Torah, is of ultimate importance in further unraveling the many intriguing mysteries swirling around the Hebrew text of the Old Testament. It's clear that Jewish scribes and priests, as well as early Christian apostles and disciples, would have gone to extreme lengths to preserve and hide any scriptural texts entrusted to them at such times when these treasures appeared to be in jeopardy. I think we can safely assume that these measures were conceived and executed prayerfully, looking toward a day when such sacred artifacts could be recovered and cherished by future generations. And it is on such a prospect that all of my discoveries and experiences seem to converge.

A More Sobering Objective

The subject of locating an older and more pristine text of the Hebrew Old Testament may be the next important task at hand, but it is not the endgame. If the original Hebrew Bible contained encoded information concerning a latter-day conspiracy conceived by evildoers bent on destroying worshippers of the God of Israel as well as other innocent people who might stand in their way, then it might be "such a time as this" for the full extent of this plan to be exposed. If the Hebrew text as it stands today reveals the general outlines of such a plan (as we have proposed it does), then an even more accurate original text, predating the Masoretic text by hundreds of years, may fill in the details and perhaps help us make clear sense out of the confusion of terror and bloodshed we now witness around the world on nearly a daily basis.

For all the reasons laid out in this book, I feel a personal responsibility to do whatever I can to raise a warning call, but obviously I'm not the only one who recognizes this perilous situation. Warning bells have been ringing from churches and temples around the world. Voices from every quarter have been frantically trying to articulate the nature and direction of highly organized and coordinated acts of violence. But there are considerable differences of opinion as to what lies behind this international campaign of terror and murder.

Encryptions in the Hebrew text suggest that we are dealing with a mirror image of twentieth-century Nazis, and judging from the nearly incomprehensible insanity of the situation, it would seem that the encrypted messages are spot-on.

Again, would a more perfect text reveal some insight as to the source and direction of this gathering storm? Possibly. But given the information we can already access, I believe it would be wise to take a much closer look at certain books in the Old Testament that on the surface seem more suggestive of containing encoded passages, such as the books of Job, Jonah, and certainly Esther. The goal, of course, is to uncover the key that reveals their true structure, just as we have with our key code in Genesis. This sort of inquiry requires methodical research, but the rewards are well worth the effort.

But why would detailed information vital to the deliverance of innocent people be hidden in the Scriptures rather than stated in the open text? For that matter, why would God hide any important guidance in the Scriptures?

I believe the answer is provided in the book of Esther. It's all about timing. Haman's plot was not revealed to Mordecai and Esther until the precise moment when Esther was in the position, as queen of the empire, to undo the murderous scheme. A premature exposure of Haman's intentions would have enabled him to maneuver around any obstacles. Instead, he was taken by surprise in the very presence of the only person in the empire with the power to prevent the catastrophe: the king himself.

In modern times, intervention will need to take place at the highest levels of political power.

WHAT OF THE APOCALYPSE?

Could it be that this generation is indeed entering that epic period foretold in both the Old and New Testaments, that time of upheaval and unveiling portrayed by the apostle John in the book of Revelation? All the evidence presented in this book certainly reinforces that conclusion, but we've heard doomsday predictions so often in the past that we're no longer alarmed by the prospect. Certainly, I have no use for fearmongering. There is enough tragedy in the world without having to conjure it up. However, it's the uncertainty about the state of the world that upsets people the most.

Even in death we take comfort from faith as we face what lies ahead on the other side of the darkness. So, too, it must be with the end of this epoch. The apocalypse portrayed by the prophets is not the end of *everything;* it is only the end of one scene in the play. But make no mistake: this particular act will end dramatically.

But what can be done at this moment to bring some clarity to a subject fraught with so much speculation? I think valuable insight can be found by further scrutinizing the many scriptures in both the Old and New Testaments that employ the phrase *on the third day.* The use of this phrase throughout the Scriptures, and the encryption *shalhoub* ("rapture" / "to draw out") that is incorporated into it, is a remarkable anomaly that deserves far more attention.

NEW CODES AND CORRELATION

In chapter 13, I mentioned that my grandfather Joseph's surname (Zangla) was a mirror cipher of a word found only in the book of Esther, meaning "the treasure ark" or "highest treasure cabinet." At the time I didn't realize that the maiden name of Joseph Zangla's wife (my grandmother) was not a real name either but rather a derogatory term assigned to her family generations earlier, in the dark days of the Inquisition. It was the Latin word *macula* ("tainted, spotted, and impure"). The term was sometimes used by Spanish and Portuguese inquisitors to mark and suppress Jewish converts (conversos) to the Catholic Church, ensuring that they did not mix by marriage their tainted Jewish blood with people of good Roman and Visigoth descent.

I intend to continue pursuing these and other avenues of investigation. There are many more intriguing codes and correlations I have not shared in these pages, and more appear with dizzying regularity. I marvel at the possibilities that yet remain, given that these intriguing codes seem to revolve around a subject that both the Old Testament and the New Testament focus on so extensively: bloodlines and genealogies.

Needless to say, I have learned from my discoveries that nothing in the Scriptures is just meaningless filler. As I've examined my own ancestry I've discovered all sorts of curious connections and information previously unknown to me and my living relatives. These involve not only the origin of family names but telltale information provided in my own DNA that helped make sense of these unusual surnames.

So far I have used equidistant letter placement to decipher encrypted information in the Hebrew biblical text. However, I've come to the conclusion that the next level of cryptanalysis might be based on letter sequencing in human DNA. A group of software experts are currently developing applications that will be able to search information based on such coding, and I'm excited about the new treasure trove of information this process may bring to light.

Even as I am honored by the responsibility I seem to have been given, I marvel at the possibilities that yet remain.

A Return to Spain

In 2016, nearly a year after our first visit to Spain, after a long and delicate process of negotiations and with the last-minute assistance of a close friend of the Spanish royal family, Abe and I were granted unlimited access to the medieval royal chapel of the Seville Cathedral, where we were permitted to take hundreds of close-up, high-resolution photographs of all the sacral furnishings as well as the interior architecture. This unprecedented undertaking marked a watershed in our quest to finally understand the direct connection between the Rocío Madonna tradition and the Spanish royal family.

Equipped (thankfully) with Latin inscriptions, the narrative and iconographical panels of the central altar in the cathedral and its associated side altars communicated the whole, nearly unbelievable story. The Rocío Madonna tradition was portrayed as having descended from all the way back to the high priests of ancient Israel in the days of King David. The central theme was the recurring dispensation and subsequent safeguarding of a mighty two-edged sword, a sword bequeathed miraculously at critical moments in history when its recipients found themselves in great peril.

Of course, the mighty sword is a clear metaphor for the Word of God, and the implication of the entire narrative was that the Virgin of El Rocío somehow held the key to the sacred repository where the Word was safeguarded.

The search continues.

ACKNOWLEDGMENTS

In my efforts to share this account of my experiences and discoveries, I have received so much vital and timely assistance from so many people, it would be difficult to acknowledge them all by name. Many are already mentioned herein or cited, but many more remain anonymous. To all of you, I offer my heartfelt appreciation.

I think it's more than obvious that without the support and, in some cases, the participation of my family, this book would not be possible.

But above all else, I must publicly acknowledge my Creator and Savior, who, despite my many limitations and faults, has allowed the details and experiences of my life to be used as a kind of signpost to point the way toward something I hope and pray will be of immense spiritual value to this generation.

APPENDIX: DECODING METHODS

The methodologies I used to unlock meaningful messages in the Masoretic text are described here and there throughout the preceding account to illustrate why and under what circumstances I chose those methods. In this appendix, however, I will do my best to supply a more systematic explanation for anyone who might be interested in my approach to the decryption process.

It is important to remember that I was not a trained cryptologist or computer programmer when I embarked on this peculiar pursuit. I took what I'd learned from my previous exposure to ancient mnemonic ceremonial devices and early writing systems and combined that with what I'd learned from my initial observations of the Hebrew text. I could see that the encryption structure reflected techniques that, although not widely known, were not unprecedented. As I've mentioned, the first principle was equidistant placement, a feature always associated with intentional design.

When I first obtained a facsimile copy of the Leningrad Codex, I went directly to Genesis 30:20–23 because it was the only place in the Scriptures that displayed a highly improbable biographical connection to me and my family (my father having six sons and a daughter and I also having six sons and a daughter).

I reasoned that if there was a message in those verses for me to uncover, then perhaps the text would address me there—perhaps even by name, since this is one way God seems to get people's attention in the Scriptures and also because ancient cultures placed great importance on a person's name. I knew how to spell my name in Hebrew, and I used the exact nine-letter spelling that appears in the Hebrew translation of the New Testament found in Paul's letters to Timothy.

I started at the first *teth* and counted forward in the text until I found the first three letters at an equidistant placement of sixteen. The rest was easy. I counted sixteen more letter positions from the third letter (*mem*) and landed on a *vav*, and so on, all the way to the final letter (*samekh*). Though I had wondered if my name could be found in that exact section of the text, it was nonetheless astonishing to find it there, as you might imagine. I knew the odds of this being a coincidence were very close to zero.

Simple though it may seem, from a strictly technical point of view there was actually a lot of decryption instruction in this first discovery:

1. Equidistant letter positioning appeared to be the primary structural feature.

2. Biographical synchronization was prominent.

3. Correlation of the primary encryption and its placement in the open text was evident.

4. Thematic synchronization was also prominent.

The first decryption program I purchased allowed me to automatically search the linear letter sequence of the Masoretic text for equidistant letter placements and then to create two-dimensional arrays based on the numeric placement of any given encryption. For instance, when the program located טימותיאוס (*Timotheus*) at an equal skip of sixteen, I could then ask the program to automatically realign the natural horizontal linear letter sequence into sixteen vertical columns, giving me a two-dimensional matrix. The prime encryption would then appear in the matrix in a single vertical column.

This step of creating a two-dimensional matrix made sense based on my experience with ancient ceremonial devices (which often employed two-dimensional matrices to position symbols and iconography). I was also aware of the belief in some early societies that information could be transmitted and received through a matrix-formed medium such as a woven textile, lattice, or web work.

It seems important to clarify what I mean by an *encryption* or by something being *encoded*. I do not use these terms loosely to mean just any name, date, word, or phrase that appears in the text at equidistant intervals. Any large text in any language will produce such occurrences randomly; these are unintended and meaningless. Such random occurrences will occasionally appear at a relatively high level of statistical improbability, but this does not necessarily mean they are intentional. When I suggest in this book that something has been encrypted or encoded in the

Hebrew text, I am referring to information that an objective scientist using standard empirical criteria would deem intentional.

An a priori condition must exist in order to positively distinguish random, statistically significant occurrences from intentional, meaningful occurrences (a priori in this case means "a condition derived by reasoning from self-evident propositions"). The a priori condition for my initial observation in Genesis 30 can be independently verified because it relies on information that is publicly available or can be made available to an objective analyst. Perhaps more important to scientists and nonscientists alike is the fact that my observations make good common sense. From the very beginning they look like intentional encryptions, and the more closely they are scrutinized the more intentional they appear.

There is nothing overly complicated about the basic mechanical operation of locating an equidistant letter sequence, intentional or otherwise. The computer program takes the search task and runs forward and backward over the linear letter sequence to determine if the task sequence is present within the selected parameters. Those parameters can include a range of equidistant placements as well as a range of text. The letter sequence consists of only the precisely ordered string of unspaced, unmarked Hebrew letters (with no regard to the five final forms of Hebrew letters). In other words, the letters *mem* and *mem sofeet* (the final form of the letter) are both treated as *mem*. This is done because the letter spacing, diacritical markings, and use of final letters are considered a later interpretive imposition on the text.

The computer program returns the text to what is believed to be its most pristine structure. Statistical results are returned automatically based on the range of parameters selected. Limiting the skip range or the text range should be done only if encryption is expected within a limited range; otherwise the statistical results will be skewed to show greater statistical significance. For practical considerations, the statistical-calculation function on a decryption program is useful only to an honest and objective researcher who can use this information as one of many considerations in determining the presence of intentional encoding.

My objective in attempting to decipher hidden information in the Old Testament was not to prove to anyone that the text was encrypted or to attempt to predict future events but rather to unravel the mystery of my own spiritual experiences. I was alert to meaningful thematic and mathematical synchronicity that appeared to shed light on those subjects. Once I had positively identified a highly improbable event, I tested the information to see how it fit into an overall pattern of information.

To put it another way, once I was certain I was holding a legitimate puzzle piece, I checked to see if it not only mechanically interlocked with other pieces but also helped to complete the picture. This decoding technique is evident in my approach to the Rocío Madonna phenomenon in the key-code matrix. The mechanical part of the process is simple and straightforward; the rest of the decryption is based on the same sort of detective work that has proven effective in solving difficult cases in my chosen line of work.

NOTES

Chapter 3: Awakening Awareness

1. Eruvin 13a, quoted in Dovid Lichtman, "The Accuracy of Our Written Torah," Bible Code Research, http://biblecoderesearch.org/Academic_Research/Torah_Accuracy1.html.

2. Devarim Rabba 9:4, quoted in "Accuracy of Torah Text," www.aish.com/h/sh/tat/48969731.html.

3. *Tanakh* is a word used to refer to the entire Hebrew canon. It is an acronym formed from the names of the three traditional divisions in Hebrew: *Torah* ("Teachings"), *Nevi'im* ("Prophets"), and *Ketuvim* ("Writings").

4. Worn copies of the Hebrew Scriptures and other religious writings are not disposed of or destroyed; they are buried. A genizah is the storage area in a synagogue or Jewish cemetery where such items are kept while awaiting burial.

5. Yosef Ofer, "Introduction," The Aleppo Codex, http://aleppocodex.org/links/6.html. I recommend the work of investigative journalist Matti Friedman, both his book *The Aleppo Codex* (Chapel Hill, NC: Algonquin Books of Chapel Hill, 2013) and his August 26, 2014, follow-up article "An Insider's Guide to the Most Important Story on Earth," in *Tablet Magazine* (www.tabletmag.com/jewish-news-and-politics/183033/israel-insider-guide).

6. Ancient Biblical Manuscript Center, www.abmc.org.

7. "Carpet pages" is a term used to refer to the pages in illuminated manuscripts, usually decorated with intricate geometric designs and containing little or no text.

Chapter 4: The Chamberlain Key

1. David Noel Freedman, Astrid Beck, and James A. Sanders, gen. eds., *The Leningrad Codex: A Facsimile Edition* (Grand Rapids, MI: Eerdmans, 1998).

2. Doron Witztum, Eliyahu Rips, and Yoav Rosenberg, "Equidistant Letter

Sequences in the Book of Genesis," *Statistical Science* 9, no. 3 (1994): 429–38, http://projecteuclid.org/download/pdf_1/euclid.ss/1177010393.

3. Elijah ben Shlomo Zalman Kremer, *Sifra De'Tzniuta,* chap. 5, 55, quoted in Rav Elyakim Krumbein, "The Vilna Gaon," *The Israel Koschitzky Virtual Beit Midrash* (in Hebrew), http://etzion.org.il/vbm/english/archive /gaon/09gaon.htm.

4. The so-called Underground Railroad was a fanciful abolitionist media invention, an allusion to an extensive network of connections and associations that established underground transportation lines no different than any other well-entrenched resistance population.

5. The chair's functions also related to divination practices; the main purpose of the central iconographic panel on the chair was to communicate, of all things, a Creation drama.

6. The chair has subsequently gone missing from the collection of the United States National Slavery Museum.

Chapter 6: The Key Code

1. Second Maccabees is a book originally written in Greek about some of the events of the Maccabean Revolt from 167–160 BC. It is part of the Apocrypha, writings that are included in some Bibles in a separate section between the Old Testament and the New Testament.

2. See 2 Maccabees 8:30–32.

3. For privacy reasons, I have shared my wife's name only in confidential settings. I also feel constrained in some cases from providing names, places, and particulars of situations and events due to the highly confidential nature of some of my relationships with many private, institutional, and government clients.

4. Elijah ben Shlomo Zalman Kremer, *De'Tzniuta,* chap. 5, 55, quoted in Rav Elyakim Krumbein, "The Vilna Gaon," *The Israel Koschitzky Virtual Beit Midrash* (in Hebrew), http://etzion.org.il/vbm/english/archive/gaon/09gaon.htm.

Chapter 7: Who Are You?

1. See Figure 11.E on page 110.

Chapter 8: Crossing the Delaware

1. See, for example, Martin Ebon, "Amplified Mind Power Research in the Former Soviet Union," *Scribd* (Althegal, 29 June 2014), www.scribd.com/doc /235393409/Amplified-Mind-Power-Research-in-the-Soviet-Union#scribd.

2. Sumanta Acharya, Mark Spector, Avi Bar-Cohen, Joe Maurer, Pani Veranasi, Ajit Roy, James Klausner, Patrick Phelan, Alexis Abramson, and Ranga Pitchumani, "Federal Programs Sponsoring Research in Thermal Transport and Applications," *Mechanical Engineering–CIME,* May 1, 2013, 61–63, www.highbeam.com /doc/1G1-329365088.html.

3. For example, Paul A. Calter, a mathematics professor and visiting scholar at Dartmouth College, shows in his book *Squaring the Circle: Geometry in Art and Architecture* (Emeryville, CA: Key College, 2006) how sacred religious meaning was compacted onto architectural features of early temples, religious monuments, and altars using geometric forms to communicate sacred understanding.

4. The Hebrew book of Genesis, widely considered one of the world's oldest extant writings, displays the most sophisticated examples of data compaction in the earliest manuscripts we have available.

5. Robert Jahn and Brenda Dunne, letter to the author, April 29, 2013, "Re: Proposed Collaboration of the Timothy Smith & Sons Research Organization with the International Consciousness Research Laboratories (ICRL) to Assess the Precognitive Power of Selected Encryption Segments of the Masoretic Text."

Chapter 9: What's Going On?

1. Obviously, I could not have engineered such data as my date of birth and the number and genders of my seven children.

Chapter 10: An Unlikely Candidate

1. Exodus 3:11.

2. Judges 6:15.

3. Jeremiah 1:6.

4. Daniel's mention of Belshazzar as the Babylonian king who succeeded Nebuchadnezzar and Evil-merodach was once thought to be an embarrassing mistake in the

Bible, as a clay tablet mentioned that Nabonidus was the last king of Babylon. However, later research indicated that Belshazzar, the son of Nabonidus, ruled as co-regent with his father, who, soon after becoming king, left Babylon for Arabia to devote himself to the worship of the moon god Sin.

5. See Haim Shore, *Coincidences in the Bible and in Biblical Hebrew* (Bloomington, IN: iUniverse, 2007).

Chapter 11: The Matrix Turns

1. Arthur Fournier with Daniel Herlihy, *The Zombie Curse: A Doctor's 25-year Journey into the Heart of the AIDS Epidemic in Haiti* (Washington, DC: Joseph Henry, 2006).

2. Juan Infante Gala, *Rocío, La Devocion Mariana De Andalucia* (Sevilla: Editorial Prensa Española, 1971).

3. Infante Gala, *Rocío,* 22–23, www.hermandadrociosevilla.com/EL%20ROCIO /PAGINAS%20OK/Leyenda.htm.

4. Haim Shore reflects the historical Jewish perspective when he states, "The Bible [by which he means the Hebrew Scriptures] uses very structured and well-focused language. Pronouncements are not coincidental. No word is redundant. No phrase is put anywhere by random selection. Words or combinations of words all intend to convey a message, and they are not there by chance alone. . . . One should not take coincidences in biblical Hebrew or in the Bible too lightly. The mathematical precision in biblical texts needs to be properly addressed and taken into account." *Coincidences in the Bible and in Biblical Hebrew* (Bloomington, IN: iUniverse, 2007), 28.

Chapter 12: The Plot Widens

1. Revelation 12:1–6, KJV.

Chapter 13: Led Every Step of the Way

1. Though there is a typically ancient and a typically modern way to write years in Hebrew, this encryption can be read as using both methods.

2. See, for example, Rachel Avraham, "Incredible Parallels Between the Purim Story

and Nazi Trials," *United with Israel,* March 10, 2014, https://unitedwithisrael
.org/strange-parallels-between-the-purim-story-and-the-nuremberg-trials.

3. Esther 4:13–14, ESV.

4. Esther 4:16, ESV.

5. Esther 5:1–2.

6. Genesis 1:9, NIV.

7. Genesis 22:4.

8. Exodus 19:10–11, ESV.

9. John 2:1, ESV.

10. John 2:11, ESV.

11. Matthew 16:21.

Chapter 14: Do Not Hide the Truth

1. John 6:47–51.

2. Hebrews 4:12.

3. Psalm 23:4.

4. Psalm 2:9.

5. Revelation 19:11–16.

6. Matthew 2:12.

7. Luke 2:34–35.

8. See Matthew 2:19–23.

Chapter 15: For Such a Time as This

1. I made the acquaintance of a professor of ancient languages. We hit it off
and he invited me to his home, where he opened up about some pretty
interesting things. He was already a full professor when the United States
entered World War II. Because he spoke several languages fluently and had
spent a few years prior to the war in Germany as a missionary, he was
assigned as an intelligence officer to the 101st Airborne Division, the
Screaming Eagles, under the command of Gen. Maxwell Taylor. He was
the first man in his division to make it onto Utah Beach alive during
Operation Overlord, the D-day invasion.

My professor friend and his small unit were ordered to move quickly ahead of the main force to gather any intelligence they could from the retreating Germans, who were having a difficult time clearing out of positions in France in an orderly fashion. Important documents, far too many to take with them, couldn't be destroyed fast enough to keep them out of the hands of the Allies. This intelligence officer and his team gathered up these documents, immediately translating those that might contain intelligence of urgent importance to the advancing Allied field commanders. Later in the war my friend was dropped into the Netherlands in a flimsy plywood glider as a part of Operation Market Garden, where he was also engaged in translating documents and interrogating German prisoners.

He told me that while he was visiting Germany in the late 1920s, he actually bumped into Adolf Hitler in the lavatory of a beer hall where the future führer was trying to drum up support for the then-struggling Nazi Party. He also told me that at the end of the war, as his intel team sped ahead of the advancing US forces, he had an even stranger encounter, one that he believed shed light on other mysterious events. The man that he said he saw was Martin Bormann, Hitler's private secretary.

2. Psalm 23:4, NKJV.

3. Charles Krauthammer, "Do We Really Mean 'Never Again'?," *Washington Post,* January 29, 2015, www.washingtonpost.com/opinions/charles-krauthammer -do-we-really-mean-never-again/2015/01/29/25447c92-a7f4-11e4-a06b -9df2002b86a0_story.html.

4. Moshe Kantor, quoted in Sam Sokol, "Violent Anti-Semitism Surged 40 Percent in 2014, Study Finds," *Jerusalem Post,* April 15, 2015, www.jpost.com/Diaspora /Violent-anti-Semitism-surged-forty-percent-in-2014-study-finds-398165.

5. Anti-Defamation League, "Audit: In 2014 Anti-Semitic Incidents Rose 21 Percent Across the U.S. in a 'Particularly Violent Year for Jews,'" March 30, 2015, www .adl.org/press-center/press-releases/anti-semitism-usa/adl-audit-in-2014-anti -semitic-inicidents.html#.V-1nhvkrJD8.

6. Barry A. Kosmin and Ariela Keysar, "National Demographic Survey of American Jewish College Students 2014: Anti-Semitism Report," February 2015, www .brandeiscenter.com/images/uploads/articleuploads/trinity-Anti-Semitism.pdf.

7. Esther 4:14, KJV.

8. Galatians 3:26.

9. David A. Rausch, *A Legacy of Hatred: Why Christians Must Not Forget the Holocaust* (Grand Rapids, MI: Baker, 1990), 231.

10. Philippians 2:15, NCV.

Chapter 16: Actionable Intelligence

1. 2 Peter 1:19.

2. Revelation 22:16.

3. Matthew 24:27, 30–31, emphasis added.

4. Malachi 4:1–6, ESV.

5. Matthew 11:14.

6. 2 Timothy 3:16.

7. Hebrews 4:12.

8. Colossians 1:15, 18, NIV.

9. 2 Peter 1:19, KJV.

10. Israel Abrahams, *Chapters on Jewish Literature* (Philadelphia: Jewish Publication Society of America, 1899), 167, www.gutenberg.org/files/13678/13678-h/13678 -h.htm.

Postscript: Things to Come

1. Claude Shannon, quoted in Stephen Black, *The Nature of Living Things: An Essay in Theoretical Biology* (Birkenhead: Willmer Brothers, 1972), 19.

GLOSSARY

a priori condition
A result or condition presupposed by experience or conceived beforehand.

Aaron ben Moses ben Asher
Renowned tenth-century Jewish copyist and scribe who refined the Tiberian system of positioning vowel sounds in Hebrew biblical texts.

Aleppo Codex
A tenth-century bound Hebrew Bible scribed in the Ben Asher Masoretic tradition. This codex was once believed to be the oldest complete Hebrew *Tanakh,* but it now is missing its Torah section.

Alfonso X
Alfonso X of Castile (November 23, 1221–April 4, 1284) was a thirteenth-century Spanish king who engaged Jewish, Muslim, and Christian scholars to translate and copy important literary works, especially the Hebrew and Greek biblical texts, into his native language. He was the author of *Cantigas de Santa Maria*. It's believed King Alfonso, known as the Marian Monarch, built the first church of Our Lady of Rocío after the conquest of Niebla in 1262. Tradition holds that "Alfonso the Wise" had the statue of the Virgin placed in the chapel at this time.

apocalypse
Meaning literally "to uncover" or "reveal." Hence the apostle John's book of Revelation in the New Testament is often referred to as the Apocalypse. The term is for this reason associated with the biblical concept of the end of days or the end times.

archetypal encounter
A peculiar encounter with an apparition, typically in the form of a universally recognized personage, type, or figure.

archetypes
Universally recognized personages, types, figures, and symbols.

ark of the covenant
A gold-overlaid wooden chest described in the book of Exodus as containing the two stone tablets Moses received from God on Mount Sinai. Also contains Aaron's rod, a pot of manna, and, by some accounts, one of the thirteen original Torah scrolls.

ba'alei hamasorah
The Jewish scribe-scholars in the sixth and tenth centuries who refined a system of pronunciation and grammatical interpretation, inserting diacritical markings and notes in and around the biblical Hebrew text without altering the existing letter sequence. See also *Masoretes*.

Bachya ben Asher
Renowned Spanish rabbi and Torah scholar (1255–1340).

Biblia Hebraica
Refers to the three editions of the Hebrew Bible based on the Leningrad Codex and edited by Rudolf Kittel.

Biblia Hebraica Stuttgartensia
An edition of the Masoretic text of the Hebrew Bible based on the Leningrad Codex and provided with text-critical notes.

biographical synchronization
Biographical information that is interwoven into a text by various methods of precise symmetrical or mathematical encryption.

chamberlain key

The key entrusted to a high court official to access the royal treasure chambers and archives. In ancient times this key was so large it was attached to a sash and visibly carried on the shoulder of the chamberlain. It is believed that later an embroidered shoulder sash alone was worn as the outward symbol of the chamberlain's status.

chiasmus

A thematically mirrored literary structure. For example, "His time a moment, and a point his space" (Alexander Pope, *Essay on Man*).

cipher code (or mechanical cipher)

Ciphers are mechanical operations or algorithms. In and of themselves they do not communicate meaning. A cipher code would be a mechanical algorithm employed to select letters or symbols that, if formed into words, phrases, or glyphs, could express intelligent communication.

codex

A book constructed of a number of sheets of paper, vellum, papyrus, or similar materials. From the Latin *caudex,* meaning "trunk of a tree" or "block of wood."

crypto-Judaism

Descendants of Jews who maintain some Jewish traditions of their ancestors while publicly adhering to other faiths.

cryptology

The science that deals with hidden, disguised, or encrypted communications, including communications security and communications intelligence.

diacritical marks

Small symbols or markings placed around letters in a text to indicate a prescribed pronunciation, accent, or emphasis.

double nail sign
The double repeat of the Hebrew letter *vav* ("nail" or "peg"). Signifying the two nails used to impale the hands of Jesus Christ to the cross.

Elohim Alef Tav
Literally the "Most High God, the Beginning and the End."

encrypted
Information or communication *intentionally* hidden or interwoven into a text or sequence of letter symbols using any number of cryptological methods. To encrypt information is to alter it by using a code or mathematical algorithm so as to make the information unintelligible to unauthorized readers.

equidistance
Literally "evenly spaced." Distant by equal amounts from two or more points.

equidistant letter skips (EDLS)
One of the encryption methods employed for the purpose of compacting intelligent information into the biblical Hebrew text.

facsimile edition
An exact photographic copy of a book or manuscript.

Gayanashagowa
The "Great Law of Peace" of the Iroquois Six Nations (Oneida, Mohawk, Cayuga, Onondaga, Seneca, and Tuscarora). The oral tradition comprised both the constitution of the Iroquois Confederacy as well as their sacred history.

genizah
Storage area in a Jewish synagogue or cemetery designated for the temporary storage of worn-out Hebrew-language books and papers on religious topics prior to proper cemetery burial.

geometric group theory

A mathematical field of study focused on finitely generated groups. This theory explores the connections between algebraic properties of these groups and the geometric properties of spaces on which they act. The theory views groups as geometric objects that can be explored in the same way as single geometric objects.

hieroglyphics

A form of writing using picture symbols representing objects or concepts. Often difficult to decipher or read without a key or lexicon.

icon/iconographic

A set of traditional symbols or forms employed primarily on thematic works of art and ceremonial and religious devices. Generally, each symbol set is expressly associated with a specific personage or ceremony. Religious icons are thus called because they incorporate one or more of these traditional symbols in their execution.

illuminated manuscript

Any manuscript, primarily in the Western tradition, that is embellished with decorative borders and other small illustrations that are most commonly floral or geometrically patterned. Gold leaf is often incorporated into the design to enhance light reflection, thus the descriptor "illuminated."

internal equidistant structure

An internal literary structure accessed via an equidistant key encryption that unlocks a two-dimensional array containing intelligent communication based on mathematical symmetry and thematic synchronization.

inverted parallelism

Upside-down or opposite positioning, order, or arrangement of letters, symbols, words, or phrases to amplify or refine meaning.

Ionia
Region of central coastal Anatolia in present-day Turkey that in ancient times consisted of the northern territories of the Ionian League of Greek settlements.

Jewish mystics
A general term referring to practitioners of different forms of mysticism across different eras of Jewish history. Kabbalah, which emerged in twelfth-century Europe, is the most well known, but much older traditions, such as Merkabah mysticism, are known to have been studied and practiced as early as 1000 BC.

Kabbalah
The ancient Jewish tradition of the mystical interpretation of the Bible, first transmitted orally and using esoteric methods (including ciphers). It reached the height of its influence in the later Middle Ages.

Karaite
A member of a Jewish sect founded in the eighth century and located chiefly in Crimea and nearby areas, as well as in Israel, which rejects rabbinical interpretation in favor of a literal interpretation of the Scriptures.

key code, a
As used in this book, *a key code* is an equidistant linear encrypted word, name, date, or phrase found in the open text of the Hebrew Bible that can be empirically demonstrated to have been intentionally designed into the text and from which a two-dimensional array can be formed based on its equidistance.

key code, the
As used in this book, *the key code* refers to the full, complex encryption compacted into Genesis 30 in the Leningrad Codex that demonstrates the various systems of encryption as well as the thematic focus of the subtext. The technical and contextual information detected from this prime or key code enabled the unlocking of additional information in other sections of the text.

Leningrad Codex
The oldest complete manuscript of the Hebrew Bible in Hebrew. It is dated AD 1008 and is currently preserved in the National Library of Russia, recorded as "Firkovich B 19 A."

Marianology
The study of the tradition of the veneration of Mary, the mother of Jesus Christ, as relates to her many symbolic and literal attributes, especially in her role as the literal mother of God and her symbolic representation as the ark of the covenant holding and protecting the Word of God.

Masoretes
Jewish scholars of the sixth through tenth centuries AD who established a recognized text of the Hebrew Bible and imposed an interpretive system of pronunciation and grammar by positioning diacritical markings next to the original consonant letter sequence of the text as well as adding interpretive side notes and commentary.

matrix
A two-dimensional array in the visual form similar to a checkerboard or crossword puzzle.

matrix-formed medium
A two-dimensional array placed or imposed on the visual surface of any medium or object, serving the function of a grid where letters, numbers, and symbols can be positioned based on various meaningful juxtapositional relationships.

Midrash
Rabbinic literature that contains various forms of commentary, including exegesis of Torah texts, stories, and sermons, which usually form a running commentary on specific passages in the Hebrew Bible. Primary purpose is to resolve matters of difficult interpretation.

mirror writing
Literally "writing in reverse order." Easily deciphered by using a mirror.

mnemonic device
An object or device (often sacred or ceremonial) used or displayed to prompt one's memory. Often incorporating symbolic and iconographical elements.

numerical equivalent
Any letter, glyph, or symbol that has an established number value.

Pentateuch
Literally "five scrolls." The first five books of the Hebrew Bible (Genesis, Exodus, Leviticus, Numbers, and Deuteronomy).

precognitive
To be aware of an event before it takes place in linear or physical time.

prime encryption
See a *key code* and *the key code.*

Primordial Order of the Virgin of El Rocío
The oldest and leading fraternal brotherhood responsible for the preservation of the tradition, pilgrimage, and veneration of the Rocío Madonna. Their private headquarters, museum, and archive are in Almonte, Andalusia, Spain.

proof document
A document retained and preserved in a secure repository against which copies or transcriptions can be checked for accuracy and authenticity.

quick-response (QR) code
A type of matrix bar code that is a machine-readable optical label containing information about the item to which it is attached.

rapture

Literally "a carrying off." The Hebrew word *shalhoub* (הלש) is imbedded by equidistant skip in the phrase *on the third day* whenever that phrase is used in the Leningrad Codex.

religious iconography

Religious symbolism often represented in multifaceted artistic forms employed to convey religious concepts and events.

Rocío Madonna

Ostensibly, a small carved wooden statue of the Virgin of Rocío venerated in the Hermitage of El Rocío in Andalusia, Spain. More broadly referring to the nearly eight-hundred-year tradition associated with a miraculous apparition of the Lady of the Dew to a hunter near the village of Almonte, Spain, sometime in the early Middle Ages.

scroll fragment

A small, often brittle segment of a larger scroll. Ancient biblical scrolls are often unearthed in a fragmented condition requiring extensive conservation and reconstruction.

Sefer Torah

A meticulously handwritten copy of the Torah transcribed under extremely strict standards. Used in the ritual of Torah reading during Jewish prayers.

Septuagint

A third-century BC translation of the Hebrew Bible and some related texts into Koine Greek. Sometimes referred to as the Greek Old Testament. One of the primary source texts for modern Bible translations.

synchronicity

The simultaneous occurrence of events or observations that appear significantly related but have no apparent causal connection. Often related to supernatural or miraculous events.

Tanakh

The Hebrew Bible or canonical collection of Jewish texts. It is the source text for the Christian Old Testament and is composed mainly in biblical Hebrew, with some passages in biblical Aramaic. The Masoretic text as preserved in the Leningrad Codex is the officially accepted version of the Hebrew Tanakh.

thematic synchronization

The harmonization or interweaving of thematic details, concepts, events, and accounts in the open text of the Hebrew Bible with corresponding or complementary encrypted information.

Theotokos

A title of Mary, mother of Jesus, used especially in Eastern Christianity. Literally "God bearer" or "mother of God."

time lock

A lock fitted with a device that prevents it from being unlocked until a set time.

time-lock code

A code, or cipher, that cannot be decrypted until a predetermined time when external future events synchronize with internal characteristics of the mechanism, or coded text.

Torah ark

An ornamental closet, usually positioned in the front center niche of a synagogue, used to store, protect, and honor the Torah scrolls. When some Jewish communities in Europe were compelled to convert their synagogues into Catholic churches during the Inquisition, they replaced the Torah ark with a statue of the Virgin Mary to represent the ark, or physical vessel, of the Word of God.

transcription

A written or printed representation or copy of a manuscript or text.

two-dimensional array

See *matrix*.

Vilna *Gaon*

Elijah ben Solomon Zalman (April 23, 1720–October 9, 1797), Talmud scholar and prominent leader of non-Hasidic Jewry in the eighteenth century.

RECOMMENDED READING

Alfonso X. *Songs of Holy Mary of Alfonso X, the Wise: A Translation of the Cantigas de Santa María.* Tempe, AZ: Arizona Center for Medieval and Renaissance Studies, 2000.

Bauer, Craig P. *Secret History: The Story of Cryptology.* Discrete Mathematics and Its Applications. Boca Raton, FL: CRC Press, 2013.

D'Agapeyeff, Alexander. *Codes and Ciphers: A History of Cryptography.* Ann Arbor, MI: Gryphon Books, 1971.

Doubleday, Simon R. *The Wise King: A Christian Prince, Muslim Spain, and the Birth of the Renaissance.* New York: Basic Books, 2015.

Fournier, Arthur, with Daniel Herlihy. *The Zombie Curse: A Doctor's 25-year Journey into the Heart of the AIDS Epidemic in Haiti.* Washington, DC: Joseph Henry, 2006.

Friedman, Matti. *The Aleppo Codex: In Pursuit of the World's Most Coveted, Sacred, and Mysterious Books.* Chapel Hill, NC: Algonquin Books of Chapel Hill, 2013.

Golden, Gloria. *Remnants of Crypto-Jews Among Hispanic Americans.* Edited by Andrea Alessandra Cabello and Sohaib Raihan. Moorpark, CA: Floricanto, 2004.

Grayzel, Solomon. *A History of the Jews.* Philadelphia: Jewish Publication Society of America, 1968.

Hernández, Marie-Theresa. *The Virgin of Guadalupe and the Conversos: Uncovering Hidden Influences from Spain to Mexico.* New Brunswick, NJ: Rutgers University Press, 2014.

Herz, Cary (photographer), Ori Z. Soltes (introduction), Mona Hernandez (afterword). *New Mexico's Crypto-Jews: Image and Memory.* Albuquerque: University of New Mexico Press, 2009.

Hoffman, Joel. *In the Beginning: A Short History of the Hebrew Language.* New York: New York University Press, 2004.

Hoffman, Joel M. *And God Said: How Translations Conceal the Bible's Original Meaning.* New York: Thomas Dunne, 2010.

Jahn, Robert G., and Brenda J. Dunne. *Quirks of the Quantum Mind.* Princeton, NJ: ICRL Press, 2012.

Nibley, Hugh, and Alex Nibley. *Sergeant Nibley, PhD: Memories of an Unlikely Screaming Eagle.* Salt Lake City, UT: Shadow Mountain, 2006.

Perry, Tim S., and Daniel Kendall. *The Blessed Virgin Mary.* Grand Rapids, MI: Eerdmans, 2013.

Pincock, Stephen. *Codebreaker: The History of Codes and Ciphers, from the Ancient Pharaohs to Quantum Cryptography.* New York: Walker, 2006.

Sherman, R. Edwin. *Bible Code Bombshell: Compelling Scientific Evidence That God Authored the Bible.* Green Forest, AR: New Leaf Press, 2005.

Shore, Haim. *Coincidences in the Bible and in Biblical Hebrew.* Lincoln, NE: iUniverse, 2008.

Tenen, Stan. *The Alphabet That Changed the World: How Genesis Preserves a Science of Consciousness in Geometry and Gesture.* Berkeley, CA: North Atlantic Books, 2011.

Ulrich, Eugene. *The Biblical Qumran Scrolls. Volume 1: Genesis–Kings: Transcriptions and Textual Variants.* Boston: Brill Academic Publications, 2012.

———. *The Biblical Qumran Scrolls. Volume 2: Isaiah–Twelve Minor Prophets: Transcriptions and Textual Variants.* Boston: Brill Academic Publications, 2012.

———. *The Biblical Qumran Scrolls. Volume 3: Psalms–Chronicles: Transcriptions and Textual Variants.* Boston: Brill Academic Publications, 2012.

———. *The Dead Sea Scrolls and the Developmental Composition of the Bible (Supplements to Vetus Testamentum: The Text of the Bible at Qumran).* Boston: Brill Academic Publications, 2015.

Van Dam, Cornelis. *The Urim and Thummim: A Means of Revelation in Ancient Israel.* Winona Lake, IN: Eisenbrauns, 1997.

INDEX

Page number references in bold indicate an illustration. An *n* in the page number reference indicates an endnote alongside the endnote number; this is followed by the chapter number enclosed in square brackets.